POP IDLE

30 YEARS ON THE ROAD AS A PROFESSIONAL SINGER

DAVE DAWSON

POP IDLE

30 YEARS ON THE ROAD AS A PROFESSIONAL SINGER

DAVE DAWSON

First published by Good Day Books
February 2024
© D Dawson
Designed by D Dawson

All rights reserved. Except for the purposes of review, no part of this publication may be reproduced, stored in a retrieval system, or transmitted in any form by any means electronic, mechanical, photocopying, recording or otherwise, without the prior permission of the copyright holder

ISBN: 9798873036790

Dave Dawson is a full-time musician and writer.
Under the pseudonym Dave Philpott, he is the co-author of the cult comedy bestsellers, *Dear Mr. Kershaw, Dear Mr Pop Star, Grammar Free In The UK* and *Dear Catherine Wheel.*

He lives in the West Country with his wife and Spanish rescue dog.

He is the only one not allowed on the furniture.

facebook.com/davedawsonentertainer

In memory of Keel Watson... thanks for all you gave me

... Also dedicated to:

Billy,
from *The Unknown Soldier*...

... and Bruce
for proving I'd have been a Shit Rock Star

...and Alan,
from *The Human Jukebox*

"I arrived at an unlikely setting for his outstanding talent - a nondescript provincial pub early on a Sunday evening of weather changing from mellow sunshine to torrential rain and back again within minutes. A clientele of three (including me) plus a solitary barmaid watched an epitome of the gifted entertainer outlined in 'It Will Be My Day' on 1971's *Aznavour Sings Aznavour Volume 2*, the fellow who's 'struggled and strived but never arrived, and I'm still unknown'. Like that person, all Dave Dawson needs is the means to get to the next level. Every element is in place: the 100% stage presence, the 'common touch', the versatility - and a voice that can cope with any given song from a vast and varied repertoire, be it Matt Monro's 'Walk Away' or a 'Paint It Black' with Brian Jones's masterful sitar passagework duplicated by Dave's supple fretboard picking. Within self-prescribed limits, he took on and resolved risky, even daredevil, extemporisations without putting off a growing crowd of drinkers, even silencing them at times like a mass bell in Madrid"

Alan Clayson
Rock Historian and Author
The Beat Magazine 2011

(You must remind me of your bank details Alan. I don't think I ever transferred the money over for that - Dave)

"This is your big break, David. How much do you want this??", snapped my new manager down the phone line.

"Not that much", I sighed, wearily. I was too old to be told off.

"So you're happy just to slog round the pubs and clubs for the rest of your life then, are you?!"

"Absolutely. It's a steady income and my diary's always full"

"You know what your trouble is don't you, my darling? You're too *lazy* to be a star!"

Foreword.
"The Man of A Thousand Voices"

My first show as a solo artist was in 1995. It was a fifteen minute spot at a club in Berkshire and I was sandwiched on the bill between a vocal impressionist and a ventriloquist. I think I got twenty quid. After petrol money, let's call it twelve.

I'd undergone extensive vocal coaching, studied jazz singing techniques for a year, and thought I was the bee's nuts. I was "killing it" at karaoke, I'd won a load of talent shows, and been described in the country's biggest entertainment paper that very week as *"definitely a young man to watch, who is clearly not short of talent, and who's determined to get it right"*.

I wasn't bad looking in those days either, and on this night was well-groomed, and immaculately turned out in a new cream-white tuxedo, custom dress shirt, razor-pressed stage trousers and gleaming patent leather shoes. The club lounge was packed, and despite the plaudits and my own self-praise, I was petrified.

The vocal impressionist was very much in the Joe Longthorne mould, and physically out of shape. I didn't consider him a threat. He was in his fifties, which to me, a guy in his twenties, made him seem seventy. He was flabby, and obviously a stalwart survivor of the *"Golden Club Era"* of the 1970s, which in my eyes rendered him dated and irrelevant. As far as I was concerned, my polished new train was being waved out of the platform to begin its trip, and his was limping into the sidings at the end of the line, all rusted up, destined for the breaker's yard.

He was straight from another gig, with minutes to spare until he was due on stage, and smashed in to the dressing room like a tornado. The house-band, also in the room, all jumped.

He was cramming three spots into the evening, all at different venues, and he didn't have a sound system. He had *"dots"* - that's slang for bespoke sheet music, usually painstakingly draughted by a musical arranger at great expense... one sheet being the drum part, one the bass, one the piano, one the guitars, and so on. The band could all "read". The dots mapped his entire act.

Fighting his way into a frilly silk shirt, sweating and stressed from being late, he caught a breath and addressed the band:
"Hi guys, nice to meet you, I don't think we've worked together before.. blasted M4 was slower than a pay and display'"
He threw a set of dots at each player, rapidly barking orders:
"Right boys... intro... hi-hat, snare, bass guitar... mid tempo... twenty four bars before I come out, then sixteen bars and up an octave... not too fast... Bobbie Vee routine... keys not too loud please... just one verse and chorus and out... must have one bar break boys, then rimshot, all in, up-tempo... Orbison is verse

chorus, out, down tempo. Vinton ... brush snare upstroke guitar"

..and on and on it went.

As he meted out his clipped cabaret commands, he strained like a weightlifter to flatten his protruding spare tyre, by squeezing a cumberbund round his belly until the clasp nearly snapped.
I remember shaking my head inwardly, and wondering,
"Who *is* this twat?" I hope I never get like that, he's off his nut"
...but he was also very charismatic. I wasn't without respect.

It was his time. I went out front and stood in the darkness, just in time to see the band fire up. They motored away alone for half a minute or so, wearing that slightly bored look that session players do, fooling you into thinking they're making it up as they go along and it'll fall apart any second, when, in fact, they're following the artist's instructions and dots to within a microbeat.

A voice, I *think* it was his, boomed over the club tannoy:
"Ladies and gentleman! Direct from the North East and making his first appearance at the Woking Club, please put your hands together for the legend, *The Man of A Thousand Voices!!*"

The band stepped up a gear. He skipped on, all clapping at the crowd, arm gestures, swinging hips, and sea-spray perspiration, gyrating like a sozzled great uncle at a wedding reception.

I looked at a sea of faces. All of their expressions asked what the story was with this fat old has-been. Then he whip-cracked the mic lead, winked at the band to check the cue, gave a thumbs up into the blackness at the back row, pretending to recognise someone he obviously couldn't see... and let his voice bolt out of the traps into *The Night Has A Thousand Eyes*. And it could've been the CD. He was indistinguishable from the real thing, only with a stronger vocal. It was almost preternatural.

Within seconds he was out of the chorus and into *Oh, Pretty Woman*, and again, with your back turned, the *"Big O"*, Roy Orbison, was onstage, at least in voice, in Berkshire. Then out again, easing into that instantly recognisable Bobby Vinton *Blue Velvet* liquid croon like it was a comfy slipper... then out into Dean Martin, Rod Stewart, David Essex and Frankie Valli before the finale - the screaming climax of Meatloaf's *Bat Out Of Hell*.

All the while, this sturdy, chunky old warhorse patrolled the stage, clicking his fingers, picking out punters with a smile, a point and a wave, and reeled the crowd into his pocket. He must have leapfrogged through thirty *"if you close your eyes it's him"* impersonations, and he left the stage to utter pandemonium.

I was suddenly aware of an ache in my jaw, only then realising that my mouth must have been open for most of his show.

With the crowd baying for more, I watched him slip into the dressing room, gather up his dots, and unbutton his shirt to towel off his drenched face and neck.

I slunk quietly in after him, all tux, slick hair and bowtie. I was absolutely awestruck. Not thinking I'd be heard over the still-wailing crowd, I hoped to be invisible. Still panting from the exertion of his performance, he accepted an envelope from the promoter, shook his hand, and asked him to thank the band for a sterling job because *"without those boys, he was nothing"*.

"I'd stop for a half" he said, sniffing his pits, "but Slough now, late spot... hope I've got time for a freshen up, I'm humming"
"Working here tonight lad?"
He'd spotted me, and was very amiable but I could barely look him in the eye. I mumbled, almost apologetically,
"Er, just fifteen minutes.. *Clubstars of Tomorrow* spot"
"Doing what lad?"
"Sinatra, mainly"
"Ah, the Chairman"

He was breathless but genuinely interested. Buttoning himself back up, he hit me with the opening line of *It Happened In Monterey*. It may as well have been Sinatra channelling through him from the grave... a Caesars Palace séance.
"Brilliant, a kid of your age being into real music.. How long you

been at it, lad?", he asked, shuffling back into his raincoat.

"Not long.. but I take coaching", I said.

I could barely hear myself. I was virtually dumbstruck by his talents, and felt as wooden as the dummy that was co-headlining. My innards were stitched tight at the thought of following him. Why couldn't I go on after someone rubbish?

He patted my head like I was a Labrador, but it was friendly - he knew the score totally. He'd probably been in my shiny shoes, in a similar quandary, many years before.

"Ah. the new breed.. Look me in the eye, lad" he said. I did.

"There it is. You've still got that spark there, lad. Try and keep that as long as you can. Don't let the circuit kick it out of ya. You've got to keep the good music going, or these clubs'll die".

He turned to the promoter.

"Isn't that right Mr. Mitchell?", he said as he stood up, wheezing. "Got to let the new pups through or you'll die!

"Goodbye all!"

He left via the fire exit, still seemingly oblivious to the hysteria still blowing up in the hall, which was all his creation.

I very nearly picked his sopping wet towel off of the arm of the now empty chair, and threw it in there and then...

...but it was the start of a thirty year journey...

...and I'm still on it.

Chapter 1.
"It's nice to be nice..."

Not too many moons ago, *The Neverending Tour* took me to Kent. Lots of pop stars complain of exhaustion after a one year run of constant shows, but they're lightweights, because like many other artistes on the bottom rung of the showbiz ladder, I've been on the road, without a break, for thirty. On the plus side, like the Foo Fighters, I also have someone to drive me hundreds of miles to gigs, fix flat tyres in thunderstorms at midnight, pay for blown exhausts, and do my Self Assessment Tax and washing. They also book me into B&Bs, dry clean my stage clothes, and haul and set up my bulky equipment, which seems to get heavier by the day at their age. They do my invoices, design my posters, chase unpaid fees, and follow up on leads. They run my diary, generate bookings, reply to emails, answer my phones, handle my security to stop people lunging at me onstage, and take care of my advertising and website. They also very kindly pay all my bills and did all my housework until I eventually got married.

...On the minus side, "they"... are also me.

Being a fair way from home, I booked a hotel and ensured that all my gigs for that weekend were in the same part of the world. It was a gruelling year, like dozens before it, with my diary straining under the weight of the two hundred and fifty dates so far packed inside… it felt almost too heavy to pick up.

I did the first job, two 45 minute spots, at an independently run pub on the Friday, and headed back for an "early" night, which, as any working muso will tell you, is around 1am, to rest my voice in preparation for the two more long bookings ahead.

Not really.

I had several pints with the guvnor, who, after over a decade of inviting me back, was now more of a mate than a client, and the hardcore locals. I got so horribly drunk that I ended up dragging the acoustic guitar out, and playing another two hour set for free at the bar, unplugged, with all huddled round in a campfire style.

It seemed like a great idea at the time, but in my defence, I knew I didn't have any reason to get up in the morning.

I tripped out of the door at 3.30am with the landlord, whose cab dropped me to my lodgings. I hit the mattress, anticipating a solid ten hour slumber, having written most of the day off. I was pretty pally with the proprietor, as I often played the lounge for him. Being a decent fellow who appreciated the shift patterns of a professional singer, he always let me sleep in for as long as I wanted and didn't hassle me with cleaners or check out times.

The bedside phone rang at *9.30am*. Still extremely "tired and emotional", as they say of paralytic actors, I grunted a grated *"hello"* into the handset, to be informed that I was required to check out by ten. I told them all was OK - I was a friend of the owner, who always extended me a few hours grace. I was told he was off for a week, and no-one on duty knew me... so tough luck.

Turfed out, I had nowhere to go. I was still blitzed, and barely awake, so took a very hard stroll up to the scene of the previous night's stupidity. It was before opening time, but the landlord popped his head out, loudly noted that I looked like an extra from the *Thriller* video, and kindly let me in. I had a bacon roll with him, chased by a gallon of black coffee so strong and thick you could have stood the spoon up in the cup.

We said our goodbyes, leaving me to weigh up my very limited options. I reluctantly decided to walk back to the hotel, and drive straight to my next destination and gig, which I'll just refer to as *"another club in Kent"*. I was probably still way over the legal alcohol limit, and I'm not proud of it.

I waded in with the gear at 1pm, and explained my temporary

homelessness to Rosie, the manageress, who said I was welcome to set up and amuse myself as best I could until kick off at 8.30pm. After I soundchecked, I returned to the bar still feeling abysmal, and asked her if there was any chance of a cuppa. That would be no trouble at all, and minutes later I was served a nice big mug of char... but mid-slurp I heard her say:

"It's a pound"

I chortled at her little joke - you'll be hard pressed to find it in writing, but there *is* a little bit of leeway in the booker/artist alliance, so long as the act doesn't push it. We're all "backroom" for those few hours we're all together. The entertainer is, if you get down to the mechanics, a freelance contractor formally engaged by the establishment to increase business. You'd never hear of a temp working in an office being charged for a brew.

"Come on, Rosie", I said. "Everywhere I play I at least get a free cup of tea.. It's just polite"

"It's a pound".

She wasn't joking. I gave her a pound.

After this rather uncomfortable barter, I parked within the club grounds and caught up with some shut-eye for a couple of hours. When I returned, I saw there was a new barmaid on. Gasping for another tea, I chanced my arm. Ah yes. Rosie warned that I might try to take advantage of the changeover in staff, and she'd passed the message on. It was still a pound. I coughed up, downed the second brew, walked into town, came back, and spotted yet another youngster manning the pumps. With a mouth still feeling like a smoke bomb in the Sahara, I said I was the singer. Please could I have a cup of tea, Sir?

"Oh yes", he said, without an atom of humour. "Everybody's told me to be on the lookout for you... it's a pound"

The exchange was made.

I forgot the entire debacle and moved on. The expression, I believe, is *"character building"*. I switched to pints of tap water, noodled on the Les Paul for a couple of hours (that's a guitar, not a man), and laid out bits of paper on the tables. Before I knew it, it was showtime. I mounted the stage, took to the mic, grabbed a can of Lynx deodorant and sprayed it under my arms.

"Come on people", I said to the audience with fake surprise.

"You don't want me stinking as much as my act, do you?"

I was about to start when a little toddler waddled up, climbed onto the boards, tugged at my cuff, and pleaded,

"Mister, can you sing *Bob Banana*?"

Racking my brains with "*no results found*" I wondered if it was a TV show or a school song. He shook his little head and said,

"No, silly... the hip shake man!"

Thoroughly confused, I looked at his dad, who said he meant *Teddy Bear* by Elvis. Just play it and I'll see what he means.

OK. Hesitantly, I played the track and strummed along.

Within seconds I was hashing it right up, losing all composure through laughter. It was the thousandth time I'd covered this number but the first time I heard the backing vocals this way:

"*Baby let me be*" (*Bob Banana*)

"*Your loving teddy bear*" (*Bob Banana*)

"Shall I do the other Elvis one, about falling in the chocolate cake" I asked the kid at the end, still highly amused.

"What's that one?", asked dad

"*In the Gateaux...?*" Then I orated to the whole crowd,

"Some people say Elvis isn't dead.. I've just killed him for sure"

"Can you sing *My Way*?", came a voice

"I normally finish with that.. I can see what you're trying to do"

My throat was as rough as a scouring pad and my voice scratchy through lack of rest. It hadn't yet warmed up sufficiently to smooth over the cracks. An apology was in order:

"Sorry I'm a little bit husky tonight"

"Husky? You can say that again. That's the sound they make when they're pulling the sleds!" shouted a punter.

Like an Olympic fencer with the little ball on the end of his sword removed... he had a point.

When a cluster of dancers linked hands in a ring on the dance floor, facing each other, I pointed to them and said,

"Ah.. if you're the skydiving formation team, great news for you...

you can stop that now... you've landed"

The first half went OK but I knew I could do better. With my vocals only running off the back-up generator after the pub lock-in, I had to pull a few alternative tricks out of the bag for the second session. Luckily, I was prepared.

"Ladies and gents", I began, upon my return. "During my break I've had a few requests. I'll address them in the order they were asked. Number one... there's no chance. I'm booked to half past eleven and I'm staying. Two... yes, you *can* have a go on my guitar but only if I can have a go on your wife. And three... I've just tried in private to shove it up there and it won't fit. Even if it did, it would be a bit whiffy if I tried to sing into it afterwards."

I got a big laugh, and an adrenaline hit that took the edge off my fatigue. Things were starting to turn for the better.

"Right then", I continued, "this song's about an old bloke who had a fried breakfast of five sausages, ten rashers of bacon, four black puddings and six fried eggs every morning for fifty years... it's called *Twenty Four Hours From An Ulcer* .. let me hear ya!"

The Gene Pitney classic was well received. I asked if there were any Buddy Holly fans in and got a got healthy *"yehhh"* back.
"I haven't got any, I'm just making conversation", I said. ".. not

really, here's my version of *Peggy Sue*. It's rubbish though so you *will* wish I'd been on the same plane as him.."

"Right, do you like Robbie Williams?"

"Nooo!", protested a front table

"He'll be devastated.. He speaks very highly of you!"

   I'd placed song sheets on the tables earlier, encouraging people to shout requests. I'd respond with a wisecrack and incorporate the gags into my act. I trotted a few out and got a good reaction:-

"Can you sing *All Day And All Of The Night*?!"

"No. If I'm not back at the B&B by twelve they'll lock me out"

"*I Saw Her Standing There*!"

"Sir. kerb crawling is still an offence in this country"

"*Can't Take My Eyes Off You*!"

"This is moving all a bit too fast for me Sir. At least take me out to dinner first and we'll see how things develop from there"

"Can you sing *In The Midnight Hour*?!"

"Did you not hear what I said three requests ago mate?"

"*Should I Stay Or Should I Go*!"

"Look, if you don't go soon you are going to wet yourself"

"*I'm Still Standing*"

"Enjoy while you can. Your missus swiped your phone while you weren't looking and she's going through your text messages"

"*Runaround Sue*!"

"Now don't be wicked, you know that only makes her dizzy"

"*Where Do You Go To My Lovely?*"

"Well sweetheart, I enjoy the trips to the cinema and the pub. What about you, gorgeous? Don't hit me fella, I'm only kidding"
"*I Fought The Law And The Law Won!*"
"I know! Appealing against speed camera fines is a nightmare!"

There are others.

As well as the comedy factor, these simple laminates ensured that I could "cater" for every punter's melodic tastebuds, be they swing, rock, country, Irish, ska, indie, Motown, 60s, disco and so on. I titled it *"The Musical Menu"* and the layout and fancy font was the same as a posh restaurant.

(I eventually ditched the feature when I realised that in some ways it was a crutch. The crowd were dictating the set and taking the wheel, when I should have been reading the room and controlling the accelerator pedal. Also, it was discordant to have a Northern Soul "dish" served up after some Country, or a deflating ballad after a banging disco tune that's got everybody gee'd up... and it backfired at a couple of gigs. Some people were using it to wind others up, with me in the firing line - like the Secure Unit after a failed escape attempt, where they demanded *Please Release Me, I'm Living In A Box, Up On The Roof* and *We Gotta Get Outta This Place,* with the recaptured "inmate" looking daggers at me. Then there was the Irish bar where some chap who'd been mugged looked fit to punch my lights out when he had to endure *Hit Me Baby One More Time*, *I Get Knocked Down But I Get Up Again* and *Aint That A Kick In The Head*.... jibes all demanded by his so called "mates"...

... but that was a long time after.)

It was a jammy night for me. All of the "orders" coming in were for pumping "floor fillers", so it became a blinding gig, as I punted hit after hit into a throng of heaving dancers. The bell for last orders rang uncannily in time with the music so I shouted:

"And on percussion!!"

The propulsion steamed through to the end of the set, and at the stroke of 11.30pm, my contracted finishing time, I took up centre-stage, and with a theatrical flourish and bow, shouted,

"Ladies and gentlemen, boys and girls, I hope you enjoyed your evening as much as I did. The kitchen is now closed. Goodbye!!"

I made my exit to tumultuous applause.

Actually, there's no such thing as "making an exit" in a lot of these places. You just start packing up. The applause was still unrelenting, and the club steward half ran, half tripped, up onto the stage, holding the mic they use for the bingo, and said:-

"Ladies and gents! I think you'll agree this young man has done an absolutely fantastic job tonight. Do you want some more?!"

"*YEHHHHHHHHHHHHHH*" replied "*another club in Kent*"

"Is this mic working??" (tap tap) "I said, DO YOU WANT SOME MORE??!!! SHOULD HE DO SOME MORE??!!"

(I don't think he got out much)

"*YEHHHHHHHHHHHH*" replied "*another club in Kent*"

Out of the corner of my smile, and inaudible to the crowd over their incessant whooping and clapping, I told him:

"It's a pound"

You won't find a clause in a contract demanding unpaid extra time. There's a little bit of leeway in the booker/artist alliance, so long as the booker doesn't push it. Encores are never mandatory, but everywhere I play, I at least give a free song. It's just polite.

"What?", he replied, completely thrown

"Tell Rosie it's a pound. Upfront"

He could see I wasn't joshing, and, probably very confused, he sprinted over to the manageress, at the other end of the hall. I watched them, silent over the continuing din, play out a fervid choreography of flapping arms, glaring eyes, spiked looks in my direction and mouths motoring quicker than a video streaming on fast forward. She then thundered across the floor towards me with a face like a stung bulldog, but as I pulled the second speaker lead out I caught her with a single, slight "*no*" head shake, and she stopped dead as if God has pressed "pause".

As I dismantled my equipment and loaded up the car, a gaggle of people swarmed around me, all asking why I wouldn't play extra. They'd all been nice, so I quoted some prime advice that the wonderful Harry Hill had imparted to me years before:

"When it's going badly, get off. When it's going great, get off."

I added that leaving on the peak of a wave and not tweaking fate on the nose by playing past it, and risking a wipe out, meant we'd have fonder memories of an enjoyable evening.

I wasn't lying was I? They didn't need to know the grimy truth.

...They all bought it.
...And it didn't cost them a pound.

Chapter 2.
"Here we are now... entertain us"

I once had to follow a technically superb but turgid eight-piece band onto a festival stage at a farm, after their hour long free-form jazz exploration gave Nytol a run for its money as a sleep aid. It was therefore down to me to try and revive "the vibe" and resuscitate a comatose scattering of idly chatting rural folk.

Within ten minutes, they'd galvanised into a herd of larynx shredding, arms outstretched windscreen-wipering village idiots. I just went out with an acoustic guitar and some three chord *Daydream Believer, Delilah,* and *Doo Wah Diddy* covers. Nobody backstage spoke to me for the rest of the day... always a great sign that you've blown another act to smithereens.

I used to fall apart while performing if I earwigged geeky guitar dweebs, who were glaring at my fingers, cupping their mouths and sniggering that I think I'll find I should have played a B7 suspended major diminutive and bent the D string up two frets in a dropped E tuning during that stanza... but not anymore.

Many of us "all rounders" may just know the rudiments of our instruments, but we're able to read and react to a crowd, build rapport, flatter to get them onside, crush heckles, navigate the set, and radically reconstruct it on the hoof, trusting our inner radar, and reloading from our ammunition store of a thousand presentable songs, to slay an audience.

I've seen astounding musicians, however, in a bursting pub, all hunched into their instruments on their stools, enraptured in themselves and each other, reciting obscure Dream Theater album tracks to omnipotent perfection... and utterly unmindful of the audience. The Hen Parties up for a boogie emptied the joint in a mass exodus, in protest, and the aggrieved innkeeper refused to pay up. I was completely with him. He asked the band if they'd ever heard of *"playing to the crowd"* and the pious bass professor fumed that his clientele were uneducated Philistines.

So what? It's a stage, not a lectern. If they're on a night out and want *Sweet Caroline* ten times in a row... so be it. They're paying our wages and keeping the venue in business, not writing a lengthy review in *Anally Retentive Guitarist Monthly* zoning in on your blatant misuse of a G minor in the Dorian scale.

I used to think that I was chomping hay in the same stables as "proper musicians"... but we're galaxies apart. I'm not here to educate, but entertain, connect, and in the words of Billy Joel, whose song *Piano Man* is the most poignant ode to the pub act ever written - and our adopted anthem:

"It's me they've been comin' to see
to forget about life for a while"...

Chapter 3.

"Ears in different time zones"

I used to play a 5pm-7pm slot at a big pub on the last Friday of every month. It was, at first glance, a weird time, but the pub was nested in the guts of an industrial estate, and the manager had devised a devious ploy. He'd worked out that if he could lure the labourers in straight after work for a swift pint and keep them distracted with entertainment during that vital two hour window where they'd normally be going home and coming out again later, then there was a fair to middling chance that he had them trapped for the entire night. *Ker-ching!*

That's six hours' solid drinking time, and, being the end of the month and therefore pay day, an *initially* full bank account. God only knows how many divorces he may have been cited in.

The jukebox is a valued ally when setting up. I've always paid close attention to the selections blaring out, as they're normally a good barometer of what's going to fire up the crowd. This one's credits were being eaten up by Ska, 2-Tone and reggae. Barring any sea-change, this was to be my set, so at five o'clock, I turned my amp right up to *"11"* and cried out:

"What are we into tonight, people?!"

"Madness!! The Specials!!", they all shouted

"What about *Two Little Birds* by Bob Marley?" I asked

"It's *THREE Little Birds* you tit!", shouted someone from the crowd, good humouredly, falling straight into my dastardly trap.

"Keep up mate!", I said "There's a cost of living crisis on! We're all cutting back! Later I'll be doing Madness *Half A Step Beyond,* The Selecter *One Minute Hero* and a song by The Fun Boy Two!"

"What about something by U.B. Thirty Nine??" said someone else, getting into the spirit

"Do some Heaven Sixteen or Level Forty One!" shouted another

"That's not Ska", I said.

"Nine C.C.!! The B Fifty Ones!"

"That's enough now"

I wellied *Baggy Trousers* into the back of the net, then revved straight into *Night Boat to Cairo,* playing the sax part on guitar, and pummelled them with two hours of the same, coloured by The Jam, Squeeze, and New Wave bands from the same era. It was a shrewd move, even if do say so. The place went bananas.

When the final whistle blew, just like *The Man of A Thousand Voices*, I was detached from the appreciative crowd noise as I changed from my stage clothes back into my *"civvies"*, in the salubrious toilets. I wondered if Justin Bieber had ever known the glamour of standing on one leg to avoid the piss on the floor.

The landlord banged on the cubicle and shouted, playfully:

"I know you're in there Dawson! Stop playing hide and seek and get your arse back on that stage! They're going barmy out there!"

"You know the rules... you should have closed your eyes and counted to ten", I replied from inside, tying my laces. "I'm spent mate, totally exhausted. I went a bit too mad out there today"

"Come on, Dave, I-", he said

"I've got no more to give", I broke in, "and I couldn't physically do it even if I wanted to. Please respect the health of your artist. The show's over and that's my last word on the subject. Just stick the jukebox back on and crank it up with stuff I've been playing"

"IT'S A HUNDRED QUID IF YOU DO ANOTHER HOUR"

I rebuttoned my shirt, opened the door and poked my head out. "Well if you put it like that...", I said

I was home by 9pm with a takeaway and a couple of cans. The high from this crazy gig, combined with trying to wind down, mixed like arms dealers at a peace rally. I was hyper, and itching to phone a couple of *"9 to 5"* friends, so as to join them on their usual start of the weekend shenanigans.

Since "turning pro", I *had* been rubbing it in a bit about long lie-ins, dropping out of the rat race, and how well I was doing, but being mates they'd taken it OK. I nearly went too far, signing traveller's cheques for our lad's holiday. I thanked the cashier for coming out and asked if my autograph was for her or if her mum was fan, and did she want a special message with it?

One friend said my head was so gigantic that I should paint it grey, fly to Mount Rushmore, and stand beside the Presidents, to confuse the American History students... while another said it was so swollen that my ears were in different time zones.

It was just banter.

Two unseen entities parachuted down onto my shoulders. The good angel by my left calmly suggested the most sensible course - stay plumbed into my armchair, watch some rubbish telly and go to bed early, waking recharged for the next night's gig.

"Don't listen to that ponce Dave!!", said the demon to my right. "You've got a hundred extra quid burning a hole in your Levis. Stuff tomorrow, it's only a working men's club. They never bloody listen anyway, they're only there for the bingo. Go out with the lads, and get so plastered that you wake up with dried kebab on your pyjamas and the memory of a wiped USB stick, feeling like your head's being tightened in a vice. You deserve it."

When I got to the nightclub my mates came bounding up like spaniels, barking excitedly. There was a karaoke competition in the big lounge bar with a £500 first prize. If I won, we could split it three ways, and move on to knocking back shots immediately

With a sideways glance to the suite in question, I viewed the tell-tale signs - a temporary stage, big screens for the words, mics, a sound system and a spangly star glued onto a backdrop.

I asked the guys why I'd want to divvy up the winnings if it was only me *doing* the winning, and whether they'd forgotten that it was my night off. Also, my voice was crusty from my three hour stint, so there was no guarantee I *would* win.

They said they'd told me about the contest so their cut was a finder's fee, I wouldn't know a night off if it ambushed me, and even if I come third, thats still £150. There's the queue - now get registering as they were running out of drinks money.

They lolloped away gleefully with tails wagging, and I joined the line. It was a hundred yards long, split 70/30 between female and male singers, and led to a bespectacled guy at a desk, asking questions, scribbling away, and giving out numbered badges.

After a minute or two, I registered disdainful looks being shot my way. Puzzled as to why, I suddenly realised with an inward groan that I was considered a "mini celebrity" in this area, as I regularly played at many venues within chucking distance.

A professional singer entering a Karaoke Competition will be as welcome as an Oompa Loompa in a limbo dancing contest or Tyson Fury sparring with a featherweight from the boy's gym just for the sake of his ego. You have an unfair advantage and will always win. I was going to be a pariah. Why couldn't I just leave it and let somebody else have a go?

A passing clubber stopped in incredulous recognition:
"*Dave Dawson?!* What do you think you're doing??"
"Er, just the contest, just a bit of fun", I replied, shamefaced.
"You know what Dave?" he replied. "I used to have a lot of time for you. I can't believe you are actually going in for this. Who do you think you are? Can't you take just *one* night off?! Loser"

Then he moved on in disgust.
"Another friend for life", I thought.

I wanted to slink out of the queue, but was damned if I did and damned if I didn't. There were now just four hopeful warblers between me and the entry form guy. I'd just tell my mates they'd better get to the cashpoint because I'd changed my mind.

No, I couldn't. The foursome in front had been one singer and three mates keeping her company while she waited. They'd now all gone and I was at the front. It was my turn at the desk.
"Yes", said the man, frostily. He'd obviously recognised me too.

"I want to enter the contest", I said, firmly. I didn't like his tone. "Are you sure?", he asked, grimacing

I lost my cool and raised my voice - this was victimisation now. "Look! I know you know who I am but it's irrelevant what I do for a living!" I shouted. "I've as much right as anyone else to that five hundred pounds!! So let's get me on that stage, shall we?!!"

He put down his ballpoint, removed his glasses slowly, glared at his writing pad, and expelled his breath evenly. Without looking up, and with more than a touch of menace he quietly replied:
"I don't really give a fucking toss what your job is, pal, and nor do the so far very patient people that you are holding up behind you... and I *don't* know who you are. The only bloody thing I'm interested in, is what you think qualifies you to be crowned *Miss Watford 1998*, you total fucking weirdo".

I turned in horror, to see my two spaniel friends flat out on the floor, clutching their chests and coughing, in hysterics.

"It was just banter", indeed.

On the up side, I was so shamefaced that I made my excuses and left soon afterwards... so the good angel *did* get her way.

Chapter 4.
Antiques Roadshow

I was contracted by Currie Motors to do the party launching their new range, at a Dealership near Richmond.

It was an invite only affair, exclusive to clients that had bought from them previously. Everybody present was stinking rich, and I overheard a TV Commissioning Editor, who I recognised from the telly talking about austerity, gloat that he'd only bought a new motor three months prior. Presumably he'd have to upgrade it at his viewers' expense because the ashtray was full.

The paperwork required *"light tasteful ambient music - artiste must be black tie"*. After giggling to myself about the political incorrectness of a "tie" typo spelt *"T-H-A-I"*, I accepted.

The contract also stated that *"light refreshments would be appreciated for Dave"*, so I made sure to skip lunch.

The car park was full and all of the roads within a quarter of a mile were heavily metered or double yellow lined. In the end, I just thought *"sod this"* and drove quietly next to the showroom.

I was all tuxed-up and purring in fifth gear economy through lounge versions of *Fast Car, King Of The Road,* and *Get Outta My Dreams*, when the Event Manager sidled up to me with saucer eyes and windmilling arms, demanding that I bring my set to an emergency stop... *immediately!*.

I was dismayed to learn that my Accord, replete with "optional extras" - gaffa-taped bumper, dinged passenger door, rusted boot lock and muddied hub-caps - was being displayed right next to "other" flagships of their brand new Honda Series...

She tersely ordered me to remove my *"V-Tecs Through The Ages"* addition to the fleet *"right now!"*. I remonstrated, mildly, saying the delay would eat into my set time considerably, as I'd be half an hour looking for a space and walking back, looking like a crap James Bond. My car would be a very long way away.

"That'll be absolutely fine!", she said.

I pulled off of the forecourt with *No Particular Place To Go.*

As for dinner, I was left with half a curled-up ham sandwich on a paper plate. The VIPs had pigged the fucking lot.

Chapter 5.
"How I stole Nile Rodgers' guitar"

Nobody can explain my life-long obsession with music. There wasn't even a record or cassette player in the house. The only connection was my dad's brother, Colin. He'd been the singer in a primitive incarnation of The Who. Alongside Roger Daltrey on rhythm guitar (before he switched to vocals), Pete Townshend on lead guitar, John Entwistle on bass, and Doug Sandom on drums, The Detours were just another covers outfit trawling the pub and club circuit in West London, trotting out Cliff Richard hits and rock and roll standards. They had nary a scintilla of the sound or ideology that would soon propel them to be one of the biggest bands on the planet for half a century, and counting. Or, indeed, any inkling of what was to come, which was perhaps why Uncle Colin left in 1963, eventually to run Thorpe Park. He's the bloke in the now world-famous photos, sitting behind Princess Diana, and William and Harry, getting soaked in the log flume.

The Detours rehearsed in my grandparents' front room in Park Road North, Acton, and in the 80s my dad found a remarkable ancient artefact in the loft. It was a dusty reel-to-reel recorder, and boxed tapes. One was scrawled with the words "*Detours Rehearsals 1962*" in grandad's handwriting. It featured three embryonic Rock Behemoths. Keith Moon joined later, which was fortuitous - otherwise there'd have been no crockery left. They were running through *Move It*, *Great Balls of Fire*, and the like. It fetched a six figure sum at Auction, so you may remember it.

Or rather, you wouldn't... because when I was a baby my dad recorded over it with me singing gibberish nursery rhymes. How we laughed playing that *Baa Baa Black Sheep* back in the attic and hearing £200,000 vaporising before our very ears.

I joined my first band, Oblivion, at the age of fourteen, with some classmates at Queensmead School, South Ruislip. We were the most famous pop group that the school had ever produced until a bunch of more recent chancers called Scouting For Girls.

We had no drummer. Our first, Paul Kingdom, had picked up my Woolworths guitar at a practice, and, within weeks, had learned Fleetwood Mac's *Rumours* in its entirety, by ear. He was fifteen. There was no chance he'd ever pick up sticks again.

I was on rhythm guitar and my best friend Ian Foster was on bass... an incredible player, and as much of a prodigy as Paul.

Paul McCauley, the school heart-throb, was our singer. His uncle was Irish songwriter Johnny McCauley, whose songs had been covered by Christy Moore and Daniel O'Donnell, to whom he'd given his first break. Paul had a great voice, a loveable magnetism, and was very handsome. He was our secret weapon.

Simon Faulkner played lead guitar. We rehearsed in his mum and dad's garage in Tiverton Road, Ruislip Manor, where we seriously lucked out. Unbeknownst to us, his dad, Ron, was a veteran of the sixties and had played in bands for decades.

He'd been a member of the seminal *Men Of Mystery*, so named for their enigmatic theatrical gimmick - no-one ever saw their real faces or knew what they looked like. They were way ahead of the curve, and Kiss, The Residents, and Daft Punk all stole the idea. Men of Mystery put sack hoods on their heads with the eye holes cut out. True visionaries, I say. All credit to them.

Like them, we had a gimmick. Our repertoire was similar to The Detours' - Elvis and Little Richard classics, and 60s tunes - so the novelty of kids playing this stuff ensured many social club gigs, fixed by Ron acting as our manager and mentor.

One day, Billy Noone, who'd drummed in the Swinging Blue Jeans, came to audition. Ron was fretting that with live dates looming, we needed percussion bedded into the band quickly.

Although, at nineteen, Billy was only four years older, he was to our eyes a seasoned old-timer... *and* he'd been in a group that had an actual hit record. We were gigging within a month.

To be a serious working musician, I knew I'd have to bin my

crap Woolworths guitar and invest in a proper instrument, so I headed to *Andy's Guitars* on Denmark Street with money saved from my paper round. I muddled around on several possibles, not feeling any of that indefinable magic. I was about to leave, dejected and still lumbered with my inferior chainstore copy, when the owner reluctantly pulled a five year old cream 1978 Fender Telecaster from a rack tucked away from public display.

His reticence was justified. It wasn't actually for sale – it'd been bought in months before by a funk guitarist I'd never heard of, to fix the electrics. He'd never collected it, and the boss didn't have room for it since taking in new stock. He handed it to me and it was mine before I even plugged it in or experienced it in my hands. When I did, it sounded like Heaven and felt like an extension of me, as all destined instruments do. I fell in love.

The owner winced a bit when I got my wallet out. He took my number, demanding that I take great care of the guitar, but not because he was bothered that I should treasure it for myself. I'd very likely have to return it unmarked when the actual owner turned up to reclaim what was rightfully his.

The call never came, and in 2015 I was watching a documentary on Nile Rodgers. He said he was so zonked on drugs in the 80s that he'd left his favourite cream Telecaster at a shop in London for a repair and forgotten where it was. I tweeted him a photo of "his" guitar, but can only guess that he was inundated with imposters sending similar pictures of their decoys, looking for a quick buck, and it was buried in the deluge.

I'm looking at it right now. Even without Mr. Rodgers' official providence - there's only anecdotal "proof" - it's still a vintage piece, worth thousands. Nile may yet respond, but it's been mine for forty years now. I learnt on it, have gigged it a thousand times, and he's not having it back... even if he does *"Freak Out"*.

For two years, we rehearsed and gigged hard, often with Ron's band, *Blues By Five.* He even paid for us to record in a bona fide studio. With its swivel chairs, screens, flashing lights and control panels, sliders and knobs, it was like being in Star Trek. I owe him a huge debt for the greatest apprenticeship imaginable.

Arriving to practice one day, after leaving my Telecaster in the garage overnight, I spotted a big dent in the back of it. I threw a wobbler and said I either found out how the damage had been done, or I'd leave the band. I didn't, so I did.

A gash in some wood, barely half an inch across - I measured it just now - changed my entire life.

I wasn't even eighteen.

Chapter 6.
"Who's a pretty boy.."

I had my first brush with celebrity on holiday in Spain in the mid-80s, whilst passed out on a sun lounger by the pool after a heavy night's clubbing. My mates and I were still very inebriated.

I was revived by sharp taps on the shoulder, and squinted up to see Michael Barrymore looming above, peering down at me.

"Oh God", I thought. "I'm still wasted. I'm hallucinating being pestered by Britain's best-known quiz show host"

I immediately went back to dozing... but felt even more rough knocks, and blinked to see that "he" was still there.

"I think you've pulled", he said

I was awake. The voice was from outside my head. It was him.

"I'm sorry?", I groaned.

"I said I think you've pulled", he repeated

"Aren't you Mich-" I began

"Look. Never mind 'oo I am" he cut in, deadpan. "Don't look behind... I said *DON'T*. Look. Behind... whatever you do... Don't make it obvious... keep cool... keep it casual... but there's a coloured bird over there, wants to talk to you"

Of course, I turned to look, as you would, to see a parrot on a perch at the other end of the pool. I was on his show years later, and he asked if me and "Polly" were still seeing each other.

Chapter 7.
"Wages, nothing, and phone numbers"

I didn't yet know that I was a solo act in a band's body. After leaving Oblivion, I wasn't out on a limb for long. A local group, playing original material, had just parted with their singer. How about auditioning for an as yet unspecified role?

I went to the scout hut in Rayners Lane where they rehearsed. They were rough around the edges - not that I was any better - but had the makings of greatness. They'd grown up together, so I was very much an outsider, and I found their language and in-jokes impenetrable. But we got on, and I was accepted into the band... where I stayed for ten years, without a line-up change.

Our sound was a hotch-potch of the bands we loved. During our tenure, we straddled "C86 indie" through to the "Baggy" and "Madchester" crazes, and out into the stirrings of Britpop. We rolled with these trends not because we particularly liked them, but because they were footholds into being "seen".

We were *A Shared Experience, Springheeled Jack* (for about a week), *Demolition Jive,* and *Nanny Venus.* It was a common trick, that NME hacks often fell for, for bands to keep changing their names to make them look new. If you stuck with the same one for too long it became proof you were failing. When Kula Shaker and Blur made it big, I still saw The Kays and Seymour.

We were one of thousands of indie groups rarely getting paid or succumbing to *"pay to play"* gigs. Bands had to cough up cash offset against how many fans turned up on the night, or sell a set number of tickets, only thereafter getting a share of the door.

It was a mucky little racket. We pulled at least eighty to one gig but the promoter tallied just twenty, so with the bar takings, and us running "at a loss". they did very well. Eventually the "system"' was outlawed after a lot of the venues got boycotted.

(*"Pay to play"* gigs are the exact opposite to what I do now. If a landlord's first question is how many people I can bring, I avoid them like glass on a beach. To have to rely on an outsider to fill your pub is not a good start. It seldom ends well)

We practised twice weekly, prolifically churning out material and recording expensive demos in studios, on top of the cost of rehearsals. Writing new songs ultimately proved detrimental. By the time they were mixed they were already old, we were bored with them, they no longer represented our perpetually shifting sound, and we'd composed better ones. We were investing ourselves in tunes no-one would ever hear, on a forever revolving treadmill... hamsters on the rolling tape deck.

❖❖❖❖

During our "Nirvana phase", our songs were written outside my vocal comfort zone and were required to be bludgeoned rather than sung. I struggled to reach notes, my voice was cracking, and my throat was sore after a long practice or gig. I was too naive to know that male singers were only fully comfortable within their natural range, be it bass, baritone or tenor.

By sheer luck I met an English National Opera principal singer, Keel Watson, who made me his pet project – at an hourly rate, of course. I'd train in his study, every Sunday at mid-day.

I'd see his partner now and again, but she was usually dashing out to go shopping, so we were just on cursory *"alright?"* terms.

A couple of years in, I was running up and down some vowel sounds and scales, when there came a tremendous crash from upstairs. It stopped me in mid "aaaair".
 "Bloody hell, Keel", I said. "You either have very deaf burglars or very large rodents. Either way, they're unwanted occupants"
 "No, that's Jane decorating" he said, dismissively.
 "Since when has she been in at this time?", I replied, bemused.
 "Oh.. Six months", he said, seeming keen to change the subject.
 "But Jane goes shopping on Sundays", I said, not leaving it.
 There was a moment's lull while he surveyed me in a way that

asked, *"What ARE we going to do with you?"*

"Look around you David" he sighed. "We live here in the sticks, miles from civilisation. The SAS would struggle to find us. Jane doesn't drive. What shops are open around here on a Sunday?"

I thought about this for a second and weakly answered:

"My God... was I really that bad?"

Another pause.

"We've got new neighbours too", he said

❖❖❖❖

During my lunchbreaks, I listened to Gary Davies' *Day To Day Challenge* quiz on Radio 1. Contestants would answer music questions and, if they got enough correct, go through to the next day, up to a maximum of five days. I loved it and applied in writing. The producer phoned the day after I posted my letter, sounding me out as suitable wireless game show fodder.

I was on the next afternoon. The guys told me not to discuss the band on air in case I made a total prat out of myself, but unfortunately Gary namechecked "Demolition Jive" in his preamble, as my letter mentioned us. I was cagey, and dodged the subject. He poked and prodded but I refused to be drawn.

It wound him up so much that he said he'd play thirty seconds of our demo for every day I got to the next round, if I delivered it to the BBC studios in London that night. I got home and our drummer, Jim, was already at my house, cassette in envelope, to drive me to Oxford Circus. Apparently, reaching twenty million listeners had prompted a change of heart in the band.

True to his word, Gary played a clip of the best track on day two, and when I got through, a full minute on day three. I dug the tape out not long ago, expecting to squirm, but it had two great hooks and the lyrics were bonkers, so it sat well in 1990!

We were booked for Dingwalls in London the week after, which Gary plugged heavily. Listeners rang the show asking where they could get tickets. On day five, after teasing out longer snippets for four consecutive days, Gary played all of *Cheeseburger,* and it sounded like it was already nestled in the Top 40.

No PR person could have strategised or bought us that week's publicity. Perversely, it was my *evasion* of Gary's questions that gave us our shot. The public were rooting for us - they'd seen this "human interest story" evolve. Buoyed by the "buzz" we'd generated, I precociously phoned some record companies after it aired, inviting them to our gig. It was already in their diaries.

Come the day, I was stoked but frightened of what was on the other side of the night. Now that "making it" was almost a dead cert, I had no idea what the future held.

Dingwalls was packed inside and out, and the queue snaked into the street. You could pick out the A&R men a mile off with their pony-tails and tour jackets rolled up to the elbows.

"This is it", I thought.

Inside though, something was "off". People were arguing with the sound guy, venue manager and barstaff. The majority of antagonists were other bands... loads of them.

An aggrieved ex-employee had waged a vendetta, booking a dozen bands onto the same night, with none set to perform. I practically begged for just three paltry minutes to play our song, because we'd assured millions of people that we would, and most of the crowd were there for us, but they were having none of it.

The record company scouts and Radio 1 listeners left the line upon learning that the "Next Big Thing", Demolition Jive, weren't on the bill, and ebbed into the night, never to be seen again. I knew I was watching what the future held.. and let go.

In the end, the guys justifiably got shot of me. After a decade of going nowhere, hanging by my fingernails to a job I detested "just until we made it", I'd run out of puff. I was also despondent at the lottery selecting which bands broke through, as they weren't necessarily the best. I was fired at a meeting, and so relieved at the decision being wrested from me that I thanked the guys profusely. We were mates again within seconds.

When I was in Oblivion, one of Ron's bandmates sermoned me that the music business was *"a living wage, then nothing, then telephone numbers"*. He meant that doing small "covers gigs" bought in a modest income to survive on, and being a megastar could reap ten digit figures... but in between netted "Sweet Fuck All". It took me a while to work out, but I got it in the end.

Our drummer, Jim Rowland, met Pete French at a club. He'd sung in Cactus, Atomic Rooster and Leafhound, who'd split in 1971. Jim asked if he'd ever been asked to revive Leafhound.

Pete jokily replied *"only every day"*. He was estranged from the other members though, so, *"it just aint gonna happen, Jim"*.

Downhearted by the news, Jim bade Pete a wistful goodbye and walked off. Suddenly, a 40 watt bulb - he was never a bighead, so didn't need a 100 watt one - went off in his brain. Thinking *"fuck it"*, he walked the five yards back.
  "If I could put a band together and recreate your album live, would you consider putting out a new version of Leafhound?"
  "Yes", said Pete French

A crack team of himself and two friends learnt the record, and reproduced it so perfectly that its father couldn't tell them apart.

Pete was bowled over, and that was Jim for twelve years - a brilliantly received new studio album, another *"Live In Japan"*, and a taste of rock stardom... all for retracing a few footsteps.

Our guitarist Marv Rice was a one-off who'd pick up a violin, harmonica or balalaika from the Oxfam shop in the afternoon, just for giggles, and be of a virtuoso standard by the end of that day. He's now one of the South Coast's most sought-after and much-loved musicians. He settled there after the band soldiered on for a bit under the name *Pelvis* before splitting up. He always seems to be in four bands at once, including a brilliant 80s duo.

I saw him in a pub once playing *A-E-A-E-I-O-U-U* by Freez, just as four people walked out. As quick as a flash he said,
  "I see we've upset a few consonant fans!"
Then he did *The Final Countdown,* playing the keyboard bit on the kazoo. Do that in your head now. It was fucking brilliant.

John Thomson, the bassist, is still one of my best friends. We toured Europe and America together, and, like Bernie Taupin and Elton John, have not had a cross word in forty years.

We just didn't write any songs.

Chapter 8.

"I'm gonna change that tune"

I was unsure of my next move. My Auntie Maureen bought me Frank Sinatra's *Songs For Swinging Lovers* to refine my tastes, and I often played it in the car as a smooth respite from my staple diet of metal and prog. It was a pleasant aid to mulling over possible futures. I'd absent-mindedly sing along, which I couldn't with my rock stuff, as it was too high for my baritone.

One day, it all clicked. I'd been contemplating how to put out the fire while drinking from the bucket of water. Sinatra was a breeze to sing only because Keel had taught me the same vocal techniques and my range mirrored that of *Ol' Blue Eyes*. It was just study fused with biology. This *was* my next move. Of course, I couldn't mimic his flawless timing, phrasing and pitch - yet - but it was still, as they say in Hollywood, *"a moment"*.

Before this lightning bolt, I'd tackled Peter Gabriel and Jim Morrison at karaoke, but they were out of my range. My new choice was the *Rat Pack* canon - Sinatra, Dean Martin, Sammy Davis Jr, and "peripherals" such as Nat King Cole, Bobby Darin and Matt Monro... and I cruised a swathe right through them.

The crowd responses were so overwhelming that I started to enter competitions. The prizes were modest, and I won a few, but it wasn't about the money. I wanted to see where I ranked amongst other vocalists. It was "Amateur Hour", as few had taken tuition, so I graduated to auditioning for theatre shows.

I'd sometimes come up against a "natural" – someone *born* with an astounding voice, and the techniques and understanding of theory drilled into me by a trained specialist for years – but it was extremely rare. They were almost a freak of nature.

There were tons of mediocre singers who *thought* they were naturals, but even the good ones would only have been half-way through the regime I'd undergone with Keel.

I also learned that the bigger the boasts, the less there was to worry about. You had to watch the ones that stayed quiet and unassuming, hiding in stairwells, unused rooms and hallways to go through their warm-ups. They kept me on my toes. I didn't make many friends, but when I did, it was with them.

The worst were the majority... those that, if told by Keel they were flat or had serious breathing or diction problems, would berate him for his "negativity" and interference in "their dream". It was their "self-belief" that would carry them to stardom. For me, music was a passion. To them, it was only a conduit to fame.

In short, they were just too lazy or deluded to put the work in. I told one that if a mechanic never read a manual and just relied on "self-belief", pouring brake fluid in the oil and fixing a clutch by adjusting the handbrake, he'd be out of a job. His comeback - that he was better looking than me - absolutely said it all.

It was still horrible to watch people with no ability, enabled and encouraged by loved ones to believe they were great and unable to fail, face hardened audition panels and get crushed. At least it wasn't on telly. That would only be a national pastime later.

As with anyone unstoppably pursuing a purpose, I thought my progress was slow and I was achieving little. I focused on the knockbacks, not the knockouts, and was the epitome of the expression *"reach for the stars and you'll still reach the sky"*.

In fact, within two short years of singing along to the radio, I'd immersed myself in my craft and played on the bill in sold out shows at Her Majesty's Theatre, The Jermyn Street Theatre, and The London Palladium, twice. At the second Palladium show, I was selected from hundreds to sing *Fascinating Rhythm* solo, as a full production number, backed by a huge orchestra and a synchronised dance troupe of ninety girls behind me. I'd appeared on telly, admittedly in a "sneeze and you'll miss it" clip on Michael Barrymore's Show, and received glowing reviews in showbusiness newspapers. One hailed me as *"potentially*

Britain's answer to Harry Connick Jr." And, the highest point personally, I'd phoned Keel to arrange my next singing lesson, to be told I'd advanced to such a degree that he must decline to train me further - I should utilise what I'd learned and become a vocal coach myself. I'd done that, too.

I envisaged myself on a future timeline where I'd already "made it" and was reminiscing about everything I'd done to get me there... and then set about *doing* everything to get me there.

❖❖❖❖

My grandmother, Nanny Venus, after whom our indie band was named for a while, was an authentic, brilliant psychic medium, who'd learned of her gift at a traveller's fair as a little girl. The fortune teller looked at her palm and closed it, saying that she couldn't do the reading because Nan was *"one of us"*.

I was out one night with work colleagues, at a classy *Pizza on The Park* type eatery, watching five vocalists singing 70s soul, contemporary standards, and The Great American Songbook, which was also my territory. They were all top notch professionals accompanied by mellow backing tracks. One of them hosted the show; a gregarious and flamboyant compere named Chris, who was about to have a huge impact on me. I'm ashamed to write that I've forgotten his surname.

There's a derogatory term in our business: *"floor singer"*. It refers to onlookers who think they're in the same league as professionals, and want to walk across the floor, climb onstage and prove it. They're the bane of our trade, and are rarely worthy of that symbolic stroll dividing the artist from the audience... and they'll empty a packed dance floor faster than a stink bomb.

During the intermission, Chris the compere ushered me into the dressing room. Apparently my work acquaintances had asked if I could get up in the second half and *"do a turn"*.
"We don't allow floor singers, they're a pain in the arse", he said, abruptly. "You're not one of them are you? What's your audition number? Which arrangement? Have you got the dots?"

This bombardment of savvy questions was an audition.
"I'm bloody not and it's *Night And Day* by Cole Porter", I said.

I told him what he already knew. It was a perfect showcase for a voice. It demonstrated phrasing, would trip you up if you didn't land squarely on the key changes, and on time, but highlight your skills if you did... and it ended on an eight second top "F" to exhibit range, power, breath control and, if you wanted, vibrato.

A few singers took the lazier route of Don Costa's arrangement, but I far preferred Nelson Riddle's, as it's less forgiving on a weaker vocalist because of its fast jumps. If you can nail it though, it sounds spot on and is far more likely to land you a job.

  Fondly recollecting *The Man Of A Thousand Voices*, I told him that the last question was a bit naughty. The singers were working to backing tracks, so I didn't need dots, as he well knew.

  His demeanour brightened, and he nodded, looking me over and measuring me up. I could almost hear the whirr of his mind working. He took a pace backwards, and folded his arms.
  "Give us a burst then", he said
  I clicked into my singing stance and let rip into the first line, but didn't make it to the second. He did the cut-throat sign to stop, gave me the once over again, and said,
  "You'll do. Save it. I've got a track for that arrangement. It's still the break, so I'll stick you on now. I'll make out you were a last minute addition to the bill. You'll be on in five".

  He introduced me humorously, saying:
  "I'd just returned from a three month run in the West End, but jogging around Hyde Park for that long had tired me out"
  "I'd toured the theatres in Scotland - Edinburgh and Glasgow and Fort William. Luckily William dropped the charges"
  "I'd been a Radiologist after having an X-Ray. The one there told me I should pursue it because he saw something in me"
  "I'd become a singer because I'd been let go of at work, and was in pieces... I'd been part of a trapeze act"

It was good of Chris. I knew he was taking a chance on me, but given our chat and my short "burst", it was a calculated one.

Keel had taught me that once the body adapts and shapes to generate a voice, it "beds in" at that setting. He'd never be breathless running for a bus. He'd fill his lungs as during an aria, and it wasn't deliberate. His training had "recalibrated" his body.

So long as I wasn't fatigued, or ill, and hadn't mistreated my voice with too much accumulative singing - very long sessions for days with no breaks - my body would always be on standby, and my voice ready to be used at full capacity... all the time.

Ideally I'd have gone on armed with *"the blade"* - the sharp clarity unsheathed when singers warm up with vocal exercises, that slices through the cobwebs in the throat. It also protects the voice, like an old car engine turning over on a winter's morning before you'd open up the throttle. But there was no time. "Blunt" it would have to be. I was in good health and hadn't misused my voice, so the differential to the listener would be minor.

I just went out and used the song as my shop window. I had no nerves, and didn't overthink it, the same as I hadn't when singing in the car those hundreds of times. I knew it inside it out, and at the end of the night, the grip on the shoulder and *"Yep"* from one of the billed singers said more than any compliment.

My friends long gone, Chris bought me a half at the bar, and asked me if I was "self-contained".

"I'm not in a band anymore, no", I said.

He laughed. That wasn't what he meant. He said if I followed his advice, I'd end up cursing him, but them's the breaks.

He said I'd need large speakers, and a powerful amp, and that would cost serious dosh. I'd need a decent mic and stands, more dosh.. I'd already be starting to hate him. I'd need cables, a long extension lead, backing tracks costing a bloody fortune and a minidisc player.. more dosh. Right, that's well over a grand spent but at least that was it.. No it wasn't. I'd need to get in the studio and record a demo CD to *give away*... serious dosh... quality photos.. dosh dosh. Business cards, coloured lights.. dosh. At the end I might despise this stupid prat I'd met at that pizza place.

"That bloody Chris, you'll say, *"costing me a bloody fortune"".*

"So why do you want me to hate you??", I asked, perplexed

"Because you've got it", he said. "After all the dosh out, it'll all come back... And then you'll love me. Because you're one of us"

I took all of his advice. I spent a fortune. Then I hawked myself around every entertainment agency in the phone directory, and every suitable venue, and waited for the work to flood in.

The work dribbled in.

Chapter 9.
"The Gunpowder Plot"

My agents were always moaning about having a stack of work that they couldn't fill, and singers like me complaining there wasn't enough. This chasm in between existed because of the "karaoke" stigma attached to singers with backing tracks, that didn't play an instrument. Although we were professionals, many venues didn't consider us as "proper musicians".

I pored over this dilemma while chilling on the sofa one day. I'd been so resolutely hell-bent on making it as a "crooner" that I was suffering from tunnel vision. It was a good vocation, but a niche market, and I'd be lucky to go full time at it. If only there was a way to expand my scope and open myself up to more gigs.

The answer was literally in my hands. I'd been meditating on all of this whilst playing Nile Rodgers' Fender Telecaster.

I cobbled together two sets of Oblivion covers I'd learnt when I was sixteen, and within a week had remarketed myself as a "guitar vocalist". I did a few sampler gigs to test the water, and hung on tenterhooks for reports to feed back through my agents.

It took about three days. The gigs started *pouring* in, and I had to quickly adjust to "crooning" not being my sole raison d'être.

After my "makeover", I asked one of my agents, the formidable Dawn, what type of music I should learn so as to maximise my appeal and attract as much work as possible.

"Oh that's easy, my dear. Fucking *EVERYTHING!*"

I aspired to emulate another of her acts. I once overheard Dawn on a conference call talking to a football club doing their next year's rota, who wanted details of a reggae musician, a Gary Moore tribute, a boogie woogie pianist and a 1940s Cockney act.

"You'll send us brochures for all those?", they asked

"No…" laughed Dawn. "Just the one. They're all Rick!"

I cherry-picked twenty songs each from disparate genres - hard rock, disco, Country & Western, Motown, Irish, ska, Britpop, 60s, and more - and embedded them into my arsenal *("ooh missus!")*. Dawn told me to learn at least one song per week, to stay fresh - advice I still heed and act upon today.

Keel had given me the upper hand, by teaching me in such a way that my voice could adapt to almost anything.

I'd lit the gunpowder. Everything exploded.

Chris the compere had been dead right about the *"dosh dosh dosh"*. Within a month, I'd banked more than I had in ten years with the band. Within three, I had to get an accountant. Within six, I had three to four shows most weeks. Within twelve, I had enough to finally jack my job in and go fully professional... which was just as well; I was run ragged, and the borders between my music and my "proper job" were blurring. I went to see a client once in my stage clothes with my gear in the car. He'd been given my business card and I'd been recommended. But it wasn't a gig. He just wanted the best deal for his contents insurance!

I've had a recurring anxiety dream since my late twenties, and I confided it to my friend, Clive Jackson, from Doctor and The Medics, who said *"oh, we all have that one!"*.

In it, I'm getting regular payslips but hardly, if ever, turning up at the office, because I'm constantly gigging. The income from my music is pocket money. My boss is very angry and tells me he can't tolerate my "hobby" much longer and it's nearly crunch time. Then an important team meeting that I can't get out of or else be sacked clashes with a gig that I can't get out of or else wreck my music career. I tell myself that the wages from my "proper job" are secure but the pocket money from my "hobby" is perilous and unreliable. I can't have both. Which is it to be?

I wake up in a start every time, for a millisecond relieved that it's just a dream and I don't have to make a decision... then I remember I've been living in the second reality for over 25 years.

Chapter 10.
"You on the motorcycle"

I had to be enterprising, and in terms of staying busy didn't (and still don't) have an off switch. I had twenty or so solid and trustworthy agents of all sizes who were piling the dates in - some booking in two gigs per year, some half a dozen, some twenty or more - but still couldn't slouch.

If I spotted a chalk board advertising singers outside a wine bar or restaurant, I dropped in a business card with a sales pitch, if they had time, then followed up with an email, and diarised it. If they were part of a bigger chain, I messaged the lot, individually.

I had most of the big social and sports clubs covered, but if I found a little one in a side street I'd swerve in even if they didn't put music on, and try and gently twist their arms into trying it out. I looked at other singers' live dates and approached every suitable gig on the list. If an audience member wanted a card, I asked why, and if it was for a club I phoned them saying I'd been recommended. If the enquirer handed them the card, I knew they'd had my name flagged up twice within a few days.

If a venue was thinking of putting music on in three months, they'd get a call ninety days later. If a club changed hands from a committee not up for live music, I'd see if the new one was.

Despite my "campaigns", I never, ever did a free gig or went to a jam or open mic night to *"show us what you can do"*. I never ever will. They can either see me at another venue or look at the live clips I've uploaded to my Youtube channel...

...and I've never cheapened my "brand" by doing gigs "for exposure". All they expose you to are yet more gigs for exposure.

Trusted agents have asked me to "partner up" with them many times, or suggested I start my own agency because I had the same resolve and tenacity... and had grown thick skin.

Some acts tell me *"I'm lucky to be so busy"*.

There's a bit in *The Blues Brothers* where they're promoting their gig and are driving behind a bloke on a motorbike with a tannoy on the car and slow down and say:
 "You, on the motorcycle.. The Blues Brothers..playing tonight"

When I'm in marketing mode, even when my diary's packed, my wife calls me *"You on the motorcycle"*. She says it quite a lot.

Chapter 11.
Acceptable for a weekday

Weekend dates were the easiest to fill in the diary, and I was yet to meet "Angus". Circus and fairground families also worked hard on Saturdays, and got married in the week, so wedding bookings from them, and pensioners' lunch clubs, were coming in... but I still had plenty of weekday gaps going begging.

I lucked onto the Jewish "day circuit", and played Monday to Thursday afternoons in synagogue halls. For audiences tiring of *Fiddler On The Roof* - their sentiments, not mine - my "crooning shows" seemed a breath of fresh air. The Jewish community was tightly woven, and you had to run a decathlon to get its trust, but once you did, it reaped decent rewards. It was also nice to return to my first "calling" of Sinatra and friends.

If I did a good lunchtime gig, I could expect to come home to a beeping machine and the LED flashing ten new messages, all from new venues that have immediately been passed my details, and followed up on the recommendation even quicker.

I received the best backhanded compliment of my career from a Rabbi, who sauntered up after a well-received concert... and it *was* that. I had an actual dressing room with bulbs around the mirror and a colossal stage with heavy red velvet curtains that yawned open onto two hundred seated listeners. He must have thought I was just pecking at scraps of work, and the Masonic function, golf club and jazz restaurant I had teed up forty eight hours later were just pipedreams. He shook my hand, and said that I was of a *"perfectly acceptable standard for a weekday"*.

I only dropped one clanger, whilst, during a spirited rendition of Dean Martin's *Let It Snow*, I stumbled over a line and declared that I had *"bought me some porn for copping"*.

One synagogue had a portable karaoke machine, which would be my surreptitious support act. I often sat socialising with a group of businesswomen in the dressmaking trade, who fed me homemade traditional food. On one occasion, Estelle got up to sing *Till*, by Tom Jones. While she yodelled away, her friends lifted their glasses to her and through a frozen grin another said:
"Estelle.. always the same, always with her mind on the business. Even when she's away from the shop she's singing about the cash register", while we heard her yowling:

'TILLLLL!"

I laughed so hard I spilt my babka.

Chapter 12.
"Special Agents"

Virtually all agents deduct 15% of the fee they're charging to the client, payable by the artist. They're acting as the intermediary connecting us to work that otherwise might not be available. It really should be that simple... but often isn't.

❖❖❖❖

I worked for an agent who dealt specifically in top end 5 Star hotels, casinos, and members-only clubs. It was a market I was keen to crack, and especially conducive to my *Rat Pack* tuxedo set, so I was overjoyed to get on his books.

Before the first gig, he informed me, quite aggressively, that under no circumstances should I *ever* discuss my fee or collect it from a venue, because this was extremely "unprofessional" with gilt-edged clients. Besides, he added, I'd be tired after a long gig and a late finish so the last thing I needed was a game of "Hunt The Treasurer" at midnight. Let him save me all that messing about, and send me a cheque, less his cut, after each job.

It's natural to do mental "post mortems" after you die at gigs, but I was perplexed here owing to a peculiar paradox. I was going down a storm at his clubs and hotels, but *never* asked back. Also, all of his clients were *"on a tight budget of £150"*... but were prestigious. I figured they were either penny-pinching toffs figuratively tossing coins at the peasant "crooner", or, as I was not yet established, I couldn't command higher fees.

All was revealed after yet another well-received show at a new members-only golf club. The treasurer, who was obviously unaware of my agent's ban on direct contact, waved me into his office after a *third* encore. He seemed apologetic as he handed me an abnormally bulging envelope, straining at the seams.

"They loved you David," he said, unable to look me in the eye... "but we can't have you back. You're too expensive. I'm so sorry".

I was baffled, both at the £150 fee seeming extortionate, and an envelope so fat the flap wouldn't stick down. I told him not to worry, got in the car and counted the cash. It came to *£600!*

It was now clear why my "considerate" agent didn't want me anywhere near the font of the hard currency. He was pleading poverty to me on behalf of the client, but charging them top dollar and pocketing *75%* of the spoils, leaving me the dregs. If it hadn't been for this accidental "prohibited transaction", I never would have joined the dots. I'd have probably wrongly deduced that, despite the applause, no repeat bookings meant that I wasn't cut out for work at this dizzy level.

I phoned him on the Monday morning, recounting what had happened. The game was up. I was keeping *all* of the money, and he could consider the extra £450 as "partial backpay" for previous swindles... and I was going to personally revisit all of the clients that he'd diddled, offering my services at a special *"75% discount"* rate of £150 - without involving him as the nefarious go-between. If he had a problem, he could sue me.

"I most certainly bloody well will!", he shouted
He most certainly bloody well didn't.

❖❖❖❖

A new agent sent me to a holiday camp in a seaside town on the North Coast. In the nineties, fly-by-night bookers were sprouting up faster than fungus. The live music circuit was booming for covers acts, and tribute acts were so expensive that I knew of one *earning more money than the singer they were copying*. These naïve cowboys thought all they had to do was sit by the phone, fill venues with acts, and pocket their 15%. If only you could set up in business as a plumber tomorrow with just a hammer.

Of course, most went under within weeks. I should have trusted my gut and declined this one, or at least asked for a non-refundable deposit or full payment upfront. That usually made them run away faster than Dracula from Ibiza.

The gig went swimmingly but six weeks later, sure enough, I received a letter. He'd got into financial difficulties and didn't have the funds to pay all the acts in one go. He owed thousands, and proposed an instalment plan to clear the monies owed.

Attached to the letter was a list resembling a classroom register, of about fifty acts on the circuit. Typical entries read:
> Don McHugh £180 - 60 months at £3 per month
> Simon Eager £150 - 36 months at £4.16 per month

Hold on, I thought. That's Simon the Stag Night Comic. He's a mate! I gave him a call:
"Wotcha Si. Did you got a letter from this joker in Cambridge?"
"Hi mate", he chuckled. "Oh yeh, that was priceless"
"What do you reckon we should do?"
"Well I dunno about you, fella.. but I got me money"
"What? You accepted the first £4.16? That's not like you, mate"

It's worth noting here that Mr Eager - a pseudonym - was a "blue" comedian in the old Mike Reid style, and far from diminutive. When I first met him, I put out my arm to shake his hand and had to hold it vertically. I remember thinking,
"Oh my God, it's a moving Wicker Man in a suit and tie. I'll bet he's got Edward Woodward and a load of farmyard animals stuffed in his belly button trying to escape. I hope the fire extinguishers are working in this club"

"Well, Dave", he began. "I rang him. I said I'd read his letter and proposal, and he was to be commended for the time and effort put into his budgetary workings. Get my one fifty ready, *all of it*, in cash, as I'd be arriving at his house within the hour"

"I'm sure you had his full attention", I said

"There was then an exchange of views David, mainly mine", he continued, "and I told him that a quid a week until I died may be alright for some but I wasn't bloody Argos. So I submitted a counter offer. If he didn't have the cash waiting when I got to his office in, now it was fifty *eight* minutes, I'd slice his knackers off with his own letter opener, bring them home in a freezer bag, chop them up into thirty six pieces and send him back one lump of his own gonad mince in a jiffy bag every month for three years. He could see just how much good they were to him then."

"That's a very well thought out business plan Simon", I said. "If you wouldn't mind, in terms of proportion and scale, how-"

"He's much smaller than me, and much bigger than you", he butted in, pre-empting me.

None of the rest us even received that *first* morsel of bollock...

....sorry, I mean payment.

❖❖❖❖

A very wealthy agent asked a friend to perform at his house for his daughter's 16th Birthday Party. This mogul had made his fortune managing some big names in the 70s, and it was more of a mansion, or a very posh Premier Inn. I went round there once to drop off some posters, and, standing chatting with him in a corridor, my curiosity got the better of me. Although it was none of my business, I asked what was in the room behind an ornate antique oak door we were stood in front of.

"I don't know", he said. "I've never been in it. Let's find out"

Quite what a teenage girl and her fellow N Sync-besotted mates would enjoy about my mate's *Stax & Motown* show was open to debate. He suspected he'd be there for the benefit of the parents.

The agent had given my friend tons of work over the years, so asked a favour for old time's sake. Could he waive his normal two hundred quid fee and do it for just twenty... as it was family.

By the way, there was a big corporate job coming up and he'd stick him in the frame for it - although he had others to choose from - on the proviso that he agreed to this "little" gesture.

My friend reluctantly took the job. Indeed, other than a few balloons and a cursory introduction to a bewildered young lady - which seemed somewhat "staged" - he didn't see anyone under mummy or daddy age on the dance carpet all evening. He rattled through *Dancing In The Streets* and, ironically, *In The Midnight Hour*, etcetera, into way past the absent kids' bedtimes...

deepening his suspicions that he wasn't there for them at all.

Upon completion of the prearranged one hour spot, he was coerced into another half hour and told not to be a "spoilsport" when he justifiably protested. He was reassured that he'd be *"taken care of"* – that's agent-speak for "given more money".

A few weeks later, after a lot of chasing, my friend received a cheque... *for £17*. The agent had *"taken care of"* charging him 15% commission on his pittance of a fee, with no bonus for the extra time. And did he get that big corporate job? What do *you* think? As for their working relationship, in the words of Cliff:
 "It's so funny.. how we don't talk anymore"

I asked my friend whatever became of the shyster. He said he'd moved to Amity, grown a dorsal fin and started eating surfers.

❖❖❖❖

I was emailed by a new agent wanting me on his roster. He'd been an act, and the words *"UK Club Singer Champion"* were boldly emblazoned on the front page of his website blurb.

"That's weird", I thought. I'd entered a few, so was clued up on National Competitions, but had never heard of this one. Also, *"UK Club Singer"* seemed an odd title. I checked online. I was

dead right. The internet hadn't heard of it either.

When he phoned, wanting photos for hotels he had "in the offing", I asked about his mysterious accolade, but he skirted the subject. Just for sport, I did more sleuthing and asked other acts and agents... There was really was no such award, and I told him.

"Look!! It means I *champion* UK club singers... OK??!!", he snapped, thoroughly sussed out.

...hardly an auspicious start to a business relationship, so I made sure we didn't have one. If you click on the website now his main act is called ... *"404 – Page Not Found"*

❖❖❖❖

The natural order should be that great acts work in great pubs and lousy acts in lousy ones, but dumps rarely tolerate diabolical artists, insisting only on the finest - those with the tools and constitution to handle everything hurled at them, except pints.

In court, you're "innocent until proven guilty". On the circuit, you're "rubbish until proven quite good", and agents will usually send their best artists into a dive bar, because poor ones would crumble or be told to pack up and bugger off. Or both.

The ridiculous dichotomy therefore exists whereby decent

artists are "punished" for their quality and fortitude, by being tossed into latrines with beer pumps and confronted by forms of life so low that bacteria would look down on them.

An agent notorious for dealing with these flophouses wanted me on his books. I agreed, but asked for a honeymoon period in his better bistros before he threw me to the wolves in his "rough and ready hostelries". He said it was the least he could do.

I received the paperwork for the first job, and in the *"other information"* section expected to read that I was being fed free tapas, and should be careful not to slip on the marble floor of what was being promised as one of his higher class emporiums.

Instead were the driving directions, in ballpoint pen:
"Turn right at recycling centre, go through breaker's yard, and onto dirt track. If you pass the building with the flat roof and boarded-up windows you've gone too far"

I didn't go too far... I didn't leave the house.

❖❖❖❖

Most acts' diaries comprise of gigs provided by agents, and those we get for ourselves. The latter are known as *"go directs"*. A guy setting up a new agency approached me in my break at a "go direct" club I'd played for years. He pumped me for tips and advice and was affable enough, so I was happy to oblige.

He said he'd love to work with me when he was ready. If he did well it would be beneficial for both of us, so why not.

When he was up and running, he phoned with *"a lovely new venue I'd go down a treat in"*. Agreeing on terms, he posted the details. I was pleased for him, and glad to land a new club.

The contract arrived. I was intrigued to see where he'd booked me, as I thought I'd already contacted every place that did live music in his area, so I cursed myself for overlooking somewhere.

My self-admonishment was unfounded. *Dumb*founded, I read that he expected to muscle in as the middleman for my *very own* "go direct" club where we'd met.. and pocket 15% of my fee.
"How is this a *lovely new venue*?" I asked on the phone after the pleasantries were dispensed with.
"Well, it is to me", he replied.
"You haven't really got the hang of this yet, have you?", I said.

❖❖❖❖

Typically, a mediocre agent will court a new client, be it The Ritz or wreckage, by initially sending them their top acts. Then, after a while, when the venue is hooked, they'll dilute that high standard with "sub-prime" entertainers, chucking them karaoke singers and any old tosh. This is because their elite artistes are now being reserved to woo and ensnare their next conquest. And so it continues, on a constant repeat cycle.

It's like dressing in your best togs for a date, then, when you're going steady, answering the door in your dirty pants. Your good clothes are in the wash to impress somebody else you fancy.

Inevitably, the original suitor will get thoroughly fed up and dump their slovenly "other half" - also losing the first wave of high-calibre artists they fell in love with. We can't even be friends for two years, because of a clause in all our contracts:

"No other bookings from this venue or via its proprietors and customers are to be taken unless negotiated through XXXX Promotions, and should they desire to book the same artist again within 24 months of the initial performance then such booking will be made through XXXX Promotions"

As one agent succinctly put it to me once:
"I'm running a business, not a fucking matchmaking service"

Of course, agents and venues fall out for other reasons. Even when they *don't,* acts and clients breach the two year rule, just to save the 15%, hoping the agent won't discover the "infidelity".

An agent I know visited one of his clubs to find his artist "in bed with them", so to speak, on stage, to dodge his commission.

"Oh, hello Jack" said the singer feebly. "Any requests?"

"Yes", said Jack, fuming. *How Long Has This Been Going On*!"

❖❖❖❖

I did one job for an "entertainment shop". *A year later*, they emailed me. They were revamping their website and required "just" £40 to update my profile and keep me on their database.

I was bored, so phoned and asked why, as an existing artist, I was paying for their window display. Also, why had I never been rebooked at that club that I did two encores in?

I was fed some script about *"going on the journey together"* and the club loving me. They and others were ready and waiting.

"OK, I'm in", I said. "Give me a repeat date at that club and you can take the forty quid for your website off my first fee"

"It doesn't work like that", they said

"Well, *there's* a fucking shock", I said

❖❖❖❖

A self-proclaimed *"entertainment guru"* offered to catapult me to the "Big Time". As a formality, he asked me to sign a Faustian pact on two sides of A4, drawn up by the Devil. Sorry, I mean, an entertainment lawyer. Actually... same difference.

To his chagrin, in an unheard of move, I actually read it first. It included, in his words, a *"standard throwaway clause"* claiming *20% of everything I earned,* including "go directs" and agency jobs where I'd already paid 15% to someone who'd *done something*. It was merely an *"expression of goodwill"*, he said.

As *"an expression of goodwon't"*, I told him and Beezlebub to do one, and stayed in the "Small Time".

❖❖❖❖

A new agent booked me for a Summer Party. I phoned him a week before to firm up details, having reserved the date and turned down other work. He denied giving me the job, and when I protested, demanding compensation, he hung up on me.

This is *classic* behaviour for a bad agent. They'll receive nothing more than a tentative enquiry from a prospective client for an event, and immediately lock in a suitable artist, telling *them* it's 100% confirmed, so they won't fill the date elsewhere. Then they'll delay sending out the confirmation contract - or won't bother at all - legally binding them to cancellation penalties if the gig doesn't happen... all the while hoping that it will.

Of course, it doesn't, and by the time you find out, it's too late to fill the date with any clients you've knocked back to honour it. The agent will then wriggle out of any responsibility by denying all knowledge of the phantom booking - there's nothing in writing, remember - or claiming the date was just "pencilled in".

As many do, he had the audacity to call again, in October, to try and screw me over a second time. His opening gambit revealed how little he knew of the business he supposedly worked in:
"Hello. Have you got any special deals for Christmas?",
which is like asking a cabbie for a discount on New Year's Eve, or expecting fireworks to cost less in the week of Guy Fawkes Night. Christmas is by far the busiest and most exhausting month in our calender, as anyone actually *in* the industry knows.

It's pretty offensive too, as it infers that any artist at a loose end must be Sunday rather than Premier League. As my mate, the accomplished Irish troubadour, Dan, puts it:
"Asking me for a cut-price St Patrick's Day gig is an insult. It's the one date I can fill a hundred times over, at a higher price"

I instantly recognised this rogue as the one that did the dirty on me in July, and called him out:
"Didn't you turn me over this year over an unpaid job?"
"Well.." he replied, obviously taken aback
"Forget about it", I said "... water under the bridge. Now.. let me

see... Special deals for our busiest time of year.. hmm".

That statement should really have put him on Amber Alert, but no. I tippy-tapped away at my laptop and pretended to rummage through some papers. Was I was looking for a file fitting his enquiry? I was actually surfing on Youtube, and scrunching up a crisp packet. This went on for several minutes, I hope.

"Ah, here it is!", I said "Yes. Christmas deals for *you*... triple the normal rate with a fifty per cent non-refundable deposit. Sorry for the delay, I couldn't find the file marked *"Amateurs and Timewasters"*. How will you be paying today?"

❖❖❖❖

"You're a bit early", said the lady, with her granddaughter in tow, as I arrived for the Garden Party. I pride myself on my punctuality, and told her I like to arrive a full hour before an unfamiliar show, to allow for niggles with equipment, logistical challenges, or other unpredictable hiccups.

"That's all very admirable", she said, "but you do know that I've booked you for my husband's surprise seventieth birthday?"
"Of course!", I said. "That's why I'm here. Even if I didn't know, the birthday cards in the living room kind of gave it away"
"Very good", she said, testily, "but today's his sixty ninth"

My prannet agent had typed the wrong *year* on the contract.

"As I said", she went on, sarcastically, "...you *are* a bit early"
At that moment, the husband came down from upstairs.

"What's all this, then?", he asked, merrily

The wife looked at me as if I'd trodden dog's mess into the house.

"Nanny? Will grandad's party next year with the singer still be a surprise?", asked her granddaughter, innocently.

"No, sweetheart" she said. "No it won't"

❖❖❖❖

"I've had an enquiry for an Indian Night and they've asked for you Dave... is that something you can handle?", asked an agent

"I foresee problems", I said. "Can you get a bit more info"

He phoned back ten minutes later.

"You're dead right, Dave. It's an Indie Night"

"For fuck's sake", I said

❖❖❖❖

Many agents have a warped sense of mileage. Alarm bells rang once when I was told a gig was *"only twenty pages away on a Nationwide A-Z"*. If you're offered a job and don't recognise the postcode and they say it's *"just up the road"*, that means it's no less than 150 miles away. If they tell you "it'll be a good day out", that means you're going to Africa.

If the pub circuit was interplanetary and you had a gig on The Moon, an agent would lull you in to taking the next day on Mars because *"well you're in Space anyway, so it's just up the road"*. If *"it'll be a good day out"*, that means Alpha Centauri.

That said, I was setting up at The Red Lion in Ashford on a Friday, a bit pissed off there were no posters up, when the agent phoned. I was about to bollock him about the lack of advertising, when he asked where in the blazes I was...

"Relax", I said. "I'm here"
"No you're not", he said. "*I* am"
"I can't see you.. Are you in the bar?"
"Yes! I'm looking at the posters next to the stage you're not on!"
"It's not *Hollow Man*!! I'm here!!"
"If you were, I'd be looking straight at you!"
"This makes no sense"
"Which Ashford are you in???!"
"Surrey"
"The job's in The Red Lion, Ashford, Kent, you wazzock "
"Oh fer fuck's sake... how far away am I?"
"Tuesday", he sighed

❖❖❖

The following dialogue occurs a lot between acts:

"Have you ever worked for *XXXX Promotions*?"

"God, that takes me back. I haven't heard that name in a while!"

"What did you make of him?"

"Well you know how it is... you meet a lot of people in this profession. There's room for everyone I suppose... there are a lot of different characters in the game, as I'm sure you'll agree"

"Christ. He owes you money too. He really is a complete c***"

"Yeh you're right he's a complete c***"

❖❖❖❖

On the other hand, I've very happily worked with more than two hundred brilliant agents over thirty years, speaking for hours and hours and barely, if ever, meeting face to face. One let me follow her car when I got lost on the way to a gig in Milton Keynes because all the roundabouts looked the same. Two decades of business and friendship, and I only ever saw the back of her head... for ten minutes.

It might take a bit of trial of error to find the right ones, but these were the "few" I'd trusted my life with...

...well, 15% of it, anyway

Chapter 13.
"Take it to the bridge..."

I was invited to the revered Stoke Park Golf Club to flaunt my wares and try to secure a highly bankable residency.

After half an hour's grovelling, and thinking it was a sneaky way out, I drove over some smooth grass, shaved to grade one, and then over a very pretty, arched bridge crossing a cultivated lake.

When I spotted a snooty golfer and his caddy gawping at this lowly serf in abject fury, I got the right hump and "doubled down", turning Metallica's *Enter Sandman* up full on the stereo, just as I passed a bunker, in an act of righteous indignation. I was affronted; as far as I was concerned, I may not have been rich, but I had as much right to be there as the "oi polloi".

The irate golfer swished his putter at me like a rapier. A servant belched up from "below stairs", driving down *their* pampered paths in a dilapidated old Honda was obviously an obscene sacrilege. I lapped up getting one over on *"The Man"*.

The bridge stopped abruptly at a striped workmen's hut and a padlocked gate to a small quarry. Puzzled, I then looked back to see that the bridge was a water feature, and muddy tyre tracks over the 18th hole's green. Sadly, there was only one way back...

There wasn't even enough room to turn the car around, so I had no option but to reverse back over the lawn ornament at a cringe-inducing 5mph, scraping both my wing mirrors on its narrow walls, and then knocking over the flagstick in full view of the rapidly gathering crowd and the events manager I'd just pitched to, who was standing in the middle distance with his arms folded, shaking his head slowly.

Goldfinger was filmed there...
...This was more like *Blunderball*.

No, I didn't get the gig, but thanks for asking.

Chapter 14.
"Chicken Evenings"

I was booked for an 80th birthday for a French lady who loved Bobby Darin and Nat King Cole. Her sons eagerly enthused that they'd hired a cabaret singer who also played *"Hen Nights"*. There was a slight mishap with the translation, and she'd looked disgusted, referring to me witheringly, in English:

"I do not think I like the sound of ziss man. What does he do to ze poor birds at zeez *Chicken Evenings*?"

In the nineties I had a Scottish agent. I'll cloak him in the name of "Angus". He's much larger than me and I don't want to upset him if he's still stalking the Earth... I also wish to continue to do so. I haven't seen him in years, so he may be on a *"long holiday"*, as they say in certain circles. I found him via our trade paper, *The Stage & Television Today,* and he gave me piles of work - mainly "Hen Nights" on weekdays - which was very welcome.

It was also an eye-opener and a leap into the murkier end of the business, working alongside smutty comedians, drag acts and strippers, for often unruly audiences. I loved it.

I was impressed by his boast that he'd given Paul O'Grady his first *Lily Savage* gig for £40 in the 80s... until I ended up working for half a dozen hen night agents. They *ALL* had.

Angus would often put on three or four shows in an evening. It seemed, to a gullible eye, jolly decent of him to appear at the end of all of them to pay his acts in person. He had to speed between venues miles apart, very late at night, barging in backstage, breathless and dishevelled, to dish out our hundred quid each, and whizz to the next one, always in a desperate rush to depart.

Angus grabbed the cash from the client before we saw it, so I suspected he was pulling a variation of the scam I'd fallen for at the grubby hands of the agent that was going to bloody well sue me but bloody well didn't. It was on a far smaller scale - no club was paying a Hen Night turn £600 for short sets of *Sex Bomb* and *Mambo No. 5* - so I didn't begrudge him. And I *was* playing the same, less plush (OK, grotty) places more than once!

Whenever I enthused about my Highlands associate to anyone in the business, I'd be told to steer clear of him. He was viewed as a *"creative entrepreneur"* who'd stitch me up, sooner or later.

In our colourful industry, the words *"creative entrepreneur"* mean "gangster". Also, if such a person tells me (if I'm stupid enough to ask, that is) that they work in *"imports and exports"*, or they shrug and refer to *"projects in the pipeline"* or *"a few things on the go"*, they're *actually* telling me they're part of the criminal underworld, so button it, stay in your own world, get back onstage and give them some Matt Monro, on the double.

However, I take folk as I find them despite what others say, and he only ever treated me well - other than maybe creaming that bit off the top... to the best of my knowledge.

He looked like a 70s throwback, with Sweeney villain hair and sideburns, always a Hamlet cigar on the go, and a penchant for shellsuits - his only nod to a later era. And he loved to hold court.

The Hen Night format rarely varied. No men were allowed in. Billed for a 7.30pm-8pm start, we'd kick off at 8.30pm-9pm, so that the club could extract as much bar money as possible from the exclusively female punters while they were waiting. The drag act would do twenty minutes of vulgar jokes and disco or showtunes, then the singer twenty more of high tempo songs like *Living La Vida Loca* and *I Will Survive* to rev them up for the stripper, who'd do ten to fifteen. Then an interval for the ladies to refuel on alcohol and swell the takings even further. Then a rinse and repeat of the same program with a different stripper.

If there wasn't a bar extension, we'd wind up before last orders, so that the by now largely shambolic rabble could glug back even more before being spewed out onto the street.

Add a £10 admission fee onto an equivalent of the National Debt chucked behind the bar, and you were looking at a very lucrative evening indeed, thank you very much.

The clutch of artists and strippers suited to this challenge and prepared to go into midweekly battle against an all-girl assault was fairly miniscule, and I felt more camaraderie within this tight enclave of rotating personnel than I've ever experienced elsewhere on the circuit. I'd instantly recognise every face (and set of buttocks and worse) in the dressing room before curtain up, and we'd swap a brief grisly tale about the last show together.

I was affectionately christened as *"Double D"*, and everything went through my P.A. rig, which was very loud and bass heavy. The strippers liked working with me because they were always guaranteed a thumping great sound as they did their stuff. A stripper with a weak sound system - I've witnessed it - just looks like a demented scaffolder with the radio on. The volume and beat is vital to the whole package (as is *their "whole package"*).

A stripper I particularly got on with wore long black curly hair, a top hat, dark Polaroids, and very little else. To a lifelong hard rocker, the inspiration was blatant. At our first gig together, I said he looked like Slash from Guns N' Roses. He grinned broadly (as he would each subsequent time we met), pleased that I'd spotted the homage, as not many others had.

I recognised him later when he found fame. He'd chopped his hair, and ditched the hat and sunglasses, but not his stage name. It was that and the smile that gave him away, but I doubted his old audiences would have made the second connection. They were looking a lot further down. His name was *"Chico"*.

What follows is an unsavoury Trade Secret that may trigger a horrible vivid image "popping up" in your mind next time you see a police truncheon, raspberry ice-pop, or burnt sausage. I'm not sorry. I've had to live with it for years, so I've been haunted by it far longer than you. I shouldn't suffer alone anymore.

Apart from a few comperes I've worked with, you'll rarely see an upright dick in a male stripshow, because the preferred method of "below midriff display" in the UK is the *"tie-off"*.

On my first hen night booking, I walked into my dressing room to find a well-toned, deeply tanned naked man sitting on a chair rubbing his willy (no, he hadn't knocked it), while looking at *"gentlemens' magazines"*. When standing "fully proud", so to speak, he shoved his engorged pee-shooter into the barrel of a giant hyperdermic syringe and slowly, *excruciatingly*, pulled out the piston plunger, creating a tight vacuum and applying maximum suction pressure. It was eyewatering, and on impulse, I even crossed my own legs in solidarity.

Then he very quickly yanked the contraption off and tied a razor thin piece of elastic *asphyxiation* tightly around the base of "where things start", as his face contorted in pain. It was like watching a porno *Blue Peter,* after the watershed.

"Er..." I said, hesitantly

"You're the new singer aint ya", he cut in, wincing a bit. "Nice to meet ya.. I won't shake your hand. Don't worry, I know it's your first one.. you'll get used to all this palaver"

I looked down again at the torture device, then back at my new work acquaintance, to see that within, no exaggeration, one or two seconds, he'd gone from stark nude to fully dressed in a naval comander's uniform - white suit, shiny buttons, medals, and peaked cap - and was slipping his shoes on. Now it was more like a magic act, or a hardcore Mr. Benn.

Before I could articulate any questions (and there were *so* many), at that very moment, the drag yelled from front of stage:

"Lay-Deeees! You've waited long enough for Dick, so 'ere he is!! He's an orificer but he aint no gentleman! Now get ready to check out Richard's Gere and welcome him on deck! Give it up for... Captain *COCKKKKKS-ON!!*

He triple jumped out of the door to a deafening Hi-Energy dance remix of *In the Navy,* and landed on the dance floor to start his ten minutes. I had a few of these hen nights in the diary, so thought I'd better grab a bit of his act to see what was what.

I spied from a slit in the dressing room door. Dozens of hyped-up women were smashing their fists on the tables, shrieking like wildcats, lunging at their prey, clapping and screeching,

"OFF!! OFF!! OFF!!", as he jigged, jogged and skipped around the entire perimeter of the hall.

Then he sprinted back to the middle, grabbed his left shoulder with his right hand, and whipped the whole outfit off from top to heel in one rip of its velcro seam, hurling it to the baying mob, leaving him in just a thong. The girls were now going crackers, and he milked it, bending into a half bow, cupping his ear and jabbing his finger towards the ceiling for them to scream louder, before tearing his kecks off, leaving himself totally naked. What the girls and I saw next were two different things. They saw a big fat wanger. I saw an elongated black pudding.

He ran to the girls seated at the back and grabbed one by the wrist, walking her briskly to the spotlight. She giggled, looking back at her mates, protesting weakly and tripping in her heels. She looked quite timid, and I later learnt that, although appearing random, the strippers' selections were often careful. As a rule, the "volunteers" furthest away wanted to be left alone and just watch, not directly participate. They'd be harmless and would play along, then dash back to their seats as quickly as possible. Those closest to the action *wanted* to be dragged up, sometimes leading to unpredictable, even potentially dangerous interactions. I once overheard a drag act say to a punter,

"If you don't want to get picked on by the stripper, sit right at the front. We call you the "Psycho Row"*. You are well safe"*

As *In The Navy* melted into an even louder *Sex On The Beach*, the pretend Captain spread a towel on the floor and beckoned the young lady to lie on it. Then he opened a bottle of sun lotion.

I'd seen enough. It was all harmless vaudeville, but just seemed a bit seedy. A few gigs in though, I wasn't even bothered.

At the end, he leapt back like a stag into the dressing room, bouncing off the walls, and looking around wildly, shouting,
 "FAAAARRRKKK!! GET ME SIZZZZZAS!"

Finding them by his dirty mags, he snipped the tight rubber ribbon quicker than a greedy celebrity opening a school fete. Yelling with relief, he collapsed into a chair, rapidly rubbing back the circulation, refilling his schlong with fresh 'O' Rhesus Positive, whilst his chocolate tan dripped to the floor in puddles.

He was right. I soon got used to the routines, the tawdriness, and the different kinds of stripper costumes and intros:

Fireman: Yellow helmet and trousers, blue coat, gas mask, foam extinguisher, plastic axe:-
"Ladies!! Here he is with his giant hose, come to break in your front door and tackle your bushfires!! Give it up for.. BLAZE!

American Soldier: camouflage fatigues, tin hat, boots:-
"OK Galz... He's been polishing his rifle all night and now it's fully extended and *YOU'LL* be the ones in the passing out parade when you see it.. Here he is.. IT'S G.I.... PRIVATE ZOUT!!!

Policeman: cap, shirt, tie, handcuffs, radio, bullet vest:-
"Girls, I've just been asked to let you know that the local traffic enforcement team are towing away untaxed vehicles in the car park. If the owner of a blue Ford Mondeo, registration G548...."

Bloody terrible night, that was too... and it *did* happen.

❖❖❖❖

It was vital for strippers to keep the drag acts sweet, and there was, pardon the pun, historical "bad blood" between a particular pair at one show. Before the second set, she knocked on the door, telling him to "tie off quick", as he was on in one minute.

When his string was tight, she went onstage, announcing that the meat feast was ready and she was going to bring him on... but just before she did, here's a funny story. It was a multi-punchline joke, and every minute or so, knowing the stripper might be going for his snippers, she kept him dangling, saying,

"So, here he is!... Oh sorry.. I missed a bit.. I must tell you this"

Twenty minutes later, his fuselage already a vicious purple, yelling in excrutiating pain and throwing himself around the room like a shot rhino, our man finally got the *real* green light, and crashed out onto the cabaret floor. As he charged past our crossdressing host I heard her call after him:-

"I said you'd do a bit extra and I hope it blows up, ya bastard... that's for what you did to me at Northgate British Legion!!"

A bitch never forgets. Jokes aside, the "tie-off" can cause blood poisoning. I can't think of a less dignified autopsy report than:
"Cause of death - Hissy Transvestite"

❖❖❖❖

I was woken by the phone at 10am, an ungodly hour for any professional singer. It was a distressed Angus. He shouted:
"Derveeee! Eff airnair.."

Oh stuff it. I can't do the accent.
"Davey! If any bastard asks, I left with you last night, OK?!!"
"OK Mate...", I said. "Why's that then?"

"Don't fuck about Davey.. just do it, OK??!!!"
Then the hum of the dead phone line.

The previous night, I did a gig for him at a football club, with an excellent drag and two brilliant strippers. The place was banging, the girls were going berserk, and the bar was carnage.

As I said before, no guys were allowed in, often not even staff, so the focus was 100% on us. We were all backstage at midnight, packing up, joined by Angus. He came to grab the dosh, maybe skim a few pounds off the top, and pay us. It was mayhem.

It was a sweltering July, and we were crammed into a tiny, boiling hot dressing room stinking of sweat, make up and baby oil, with a horde of women, all whazzed up on four hours of Chardonnay and Vodka and Red Bull, literally screaming outside and thumping on the locked door to be let in for "autographs".

Have you ever seen any of those George Romero films where the last remaining humans are barricaded into the last vacant room on Earth, surrounded by hundreds of groaning zombies splintering the doors and punching holes in the plaster?

Well this was similar, only with added stilletos, handbags and micro skirts. In the films though, the zombies were trying to get in to devour human flesh, whereas these girls desperate to reach us were trying to get- Actually, scrub that. The situations have more parallels than I originally thought. Eventually *our* "Undead" were picked off one by one, not by the traditional method of removing the head or destroying the brain, but taxis.

The strippers and drag escaped, leaving just me, Angus, and a barmaid with the keys to lock up. She was totally soused from serving booze and being bought "one for yourself" all night, and I knew he fancied her. They disappeared to another room and "had relations", so I put my blinkers on, loaded up, and slunk off home... and the next morning I got that phone call.

He rang back a few days later, a lot less flustered, with more work for me, and I asked him if I'd still "given him a lift the previous Friday". He chuckled and said it didn't matter now. When I pushed gently for him to elaborate, he filled in the gaps.

He'd left at 2am with the blotto barmaid slumped in the back of his car, and she'd somehow directed him to where she lived, to be dropped off. When he went to pull up at her address, he spotted, lit by the hallway, a gigantic husband outside her open front door, wearing tracksuit bottoms, no shoes, and an enraged expression on his beetroot red face... and wielding a cricket bat.

Angus saw no bowler or wickets in the immediate area. To be fair, though, it *was* dark. He therefore feared that the furious spouse's motive for being thus equipped at such an unsocial hour wasn't nocturnal cricket... so he put his head down, floored the accelerator and skidded round the block.

He arrived back at the same spot to find that not much had changed from the previous situation half a minute earlier... so he drove round the block again.

Angus said that on the third lap the guy had swapped the bat from one hand to the other, which didn't actually constitute a great alteration in the overall scheme of things... so he drove round again. Upon reaching the same spot a *fourth* time, the man was appearing to register an interest in this suspicious vehicle playing on loop on his estate, by following its path with his large swivelling shaved head and the tip of his bat.

But as Angus began his fifth circuit, a plan was formulating in his wretched mind. By the time he pulled up at the address, it was ready for execution. He wound down the window, motioned the would-be assailant over, and in an exasperated tone asked:
"For fuck's sake mate... do you know where Corfe Towers is?"
"You're in it", came the unfriendly reply.

"Thank Christ for that!", said Angus in fake relief. "I've got this pissed up woman in the back of my cab, I've driven round the block ten times and I can't get a word of sense out of her. My controller's going ballistic... I've got another three pick ups and an airport run to do, and if I don't unload her on her poor old man soon I'll be looking for a new cab firm in the morning. Am I anywhere near number ten, pal?? I'm in the shit here!!"

The big man's face softened from furious into a grateful smile. Dropping the cricket bat, he opened the rear door, spilling his inebriated wife gently onto the pavement, and said:

"Mate, you're a lifesaver! This is the place! Sorry to scare you with the bat but she was working some damned hen night and I thought she'd copped off with a bloody stripper or someone. The guy running these shows is a right gangster, by all accounts. Thanks so much pal. I'm really really sorry she's put you out"

"No worries pal", said Angus, ignoring the personal insult

"How much do I owe you?", asked the now unarmed husband.

Angus pretended to make a mental calculation. Incorporating the cost for the insult into the final figure, he said,

"It's two miles from the club but I've clocked up more driving round the flats ten times. I've had grief from my controller, and you may have made my prebooked passenger miss his plane."

"I understand mate", said the husband, fishing into his trackie pockets for cash or coins. "No worries. Will a tenner cover it?"

"Call it fifteen and we'll say no more", said Angus

"I've only got a twenty", said the husband, handing out a crumpled note. "Can you break it?"

"Really sorry fella" sighed Angus. "I've done all my change"

"Take it", said the husband, hesitantly. "I'm just happy to get her back untouched"

Angus snatched it. "You're a diamond..."

Angus had been jittery the next day, and I *was* required as the alibi, but by now he'd figured he was in the clear.

As I said before, Angus did love to hold court at his events, and for the next few years, at the end of every night I worked for him, I'd get very accustomed to a drunken bellow of:

"DAVEY!! DAVEY!! GET DAVEY!!"

I'd bound up like an obedient puppy, and even if I'd been in my dressing room, I knew the scene that was going to greet me, as it was the same every time. Angus, shellsuited, puffing on a Hamlet, circled by a group of new, invariably women, punters.

I'd break the circle and say,

"Yes, Angus?", acting all bewildered, as if I had no idea what he wanted because this had definitely *never* happened before.

Angus would look around at his audience, then at me, and say:

"Everybody.. this is is young Davey, your singer from earlier. He tells it far better than me. Now, Davey.. tell these lovely people about the time that guy paid me to shag his wife"

Chapter 15.
"Don't make a meal of it..."

I was booked into an award-winning Gastropub for a lunchtime gig. It was a converted farmhouse and reeked of prosperity, but I arrived to find it emptier than an election promise.

I was a "crowd-puller" in the area, so they must have assumed they didn't have to tell anyone I was coming. There were no posters or advertising, and when the headwaiter complained that I hadn't bought a following, I had to bite my lip or else say that not even Ed Sheeran's hardcore supporters would be "following" him into a restaurant asking £25 for a prawn cocktail.

By showtime, they'd seated a table for four out of a possible one hundred and fifty, who completely ignored me. I pulled off into a set I call *The London Taxi* - you just trudge along with the meter running and the passengers refuse to talk to you.

In my break, the chef ambled up and asked to take my order. I said thanks, but I already had a ready meal at home. He said to forget the frozen junk - he was happy to knock me something up. It wasn't every day you had a Michelin Chef twiddling his thumbs with no cooking to do, so I should grab the chance.

I said I was sorry to sound tight, but I'd seen the prices and I'd stick with my microwave Lasagne. He looked around the empty room in a comedy sketch fashion, as if ensuring nobody was listening, then whispered gruffly out of the side of his mouth:

"Let's just call it a tenner. If the boss moans, I'll blame the till"

I wasn't that hungry, but it was a once in a lifetime offer, and would only dent my fee. I had the venison and the duck, and they uncorked a Merlot which I didn't touch because I was on duty. Then I got back in my invisible taxi, setting off into a second half of singing and nattering to myself with only cutlery for applause.

When the postman dropped the mail off, I laughed and mock-pleaded with him not to leave as he'd halve the audience.

The lone quartet finished their desserts. In a last ditch effort to keep them in, I asked if anyone had any requests. Soon after, I was heartened to see a waiter place a folded piece of paper by my amp. An answered prayer! I'll make a meal of this, I thought. A personal song will detain them ten minutes if I do a long intro...

...but it wasn't a request. It was a *bill*, and the porcelain dish it arrived on should have been a dead giveaway. There was a note with it, scribbled with the words,

"Entertainer - 10% Discount".

Oh, you spoil me! What better way to salvage a dismal turnout and money spent on an entertainer than to claw as much as possible back from the entertainer *himself*. Genius.

That chef knew full well that a tenner meant *£10* in colloquial Olde English, and played it like a hustle. It was a sleazy move.

The damage including VAT exceeded my fee. I was in the red. Most of it was swallowed up by the Red that I hadn't. I wondered if Rosie, from *"another club in Kent"* held a stake in this shack.

I was livid, but coughed up. I went home, famished, to my M&S Italian. My "bargain brunch" wouldn't have filled an Action Man.

❖❖❖❖

My mate Sean played a wedding at a castle, with more money pumped into it than a bank bail-out. The cake cost £5,000, and the sit-down meal £150 per head, catering for a populace that made the crowd scenes in *Gandhi* look like a get-together during Lockdown. The DJ was delivered by chopper from Ayia Napa and there were so many flowers in Reception at a tenner a petal that Sean half-expected to find David Attenborough crouching beside them doing a whispered piece to camera.

Sean was engaged to mingle round the diners with a radio mic singing love songs until desserts and coffee, for the sum of... drum-roll... *£250!* It was a good wedge for a bog standard club, but placed his worth here as less than a plate of vol-au-vents.

The job done, he found the Best Men for his fee, who shook his hand limply, not even looking at him while talking to a guest. Nor was Sean thanked for a pucker job. The money bag was *£20 light*, and so began the haggle tennis match, with both parties slamming ever more snarky backhands at each other over what was, to the budget, not even a penny behind the chaise longe.

As they argued, a tipsy bridesmaid waltzed past shoving a slab of icing into her face, and Sean shouted:
"You're quibbling over twenty quid and she's just *eaten* forty!!"

The Best Man dug his heels in, leaving a highly rankled Sean throwing down his racquet and stamping off court with the slashed fee in his pocket, angrier than John McEnroe.

On his way out he spied a door ajar to an empty ante-room. In it was a table filled with a savoury bounty - the buffet for later. He grabbed a gold-edged plate and piled it so high with caviar, fresh salmon, and Wagyu beef that snow formed on top and a Sherpa tried to put a flag in it. He scoffed the lot and then went back for seconds. Then smaller thirds.

Advantage, fat Sean.

Chapter 16.
"Die Another Day"

A poor lady died at a lunch club whilst I was performing. Not one to miss out on a new client, an off-duty undertaker offered to call his hearse out and take the deceased straight to his Chapel of Rest, so as to cut out the middle man. All sorts of protocols were probably flouted, but I swear that's what happened!

I was told to finish off the show "as a mark of respect"... but I'd been paid in advance, so I think they wanted their hour's worth.

At the end of the gig the undertaker gleefully ran up and shook my hand vigorously, grinning broadly.
 "That was absolutely brilliant!", he gushed. "Please tell me you're playing here again!"

I'm not sure if he liked my set or if I was just great for business.

❖❖❖❖

A lady at a companion club suffered a coughing fit during my *Molly Malone,* which, as bad luck would have it, she'd requested. As she was rushed out on a trolley, I realised with horror that her departure synchronised perfectly with my singing:
 "She died of a fever and no one could save her"

❖❖❖❖

A heavily perspiring, overweight punter of about sixty dropped like a boulder in front of me at an Irish bar in West London, while jigging about to my *diddly-dee* version of *Whiskey In The Jar*. He was pronounced dead on the spot by an ambulance worker on a night off, who revived him with mouth-to-mouth.

"Lazarus" was completely unappreciative of being resurrected, and the paramedic was furious, both at his ingratitude and his refusal to accept his stern advice to go home and rest.

He was in my face three pints of Guinness and an hour later shouting for me to play *The Irish Rover*, which, if anything, was about 100mph faster than the song that temporarily killed him.
I looked over at the NHS hero and mouthed,
"Shall I?"

❖❖❖❖

I played a Monday night after-dinner cabaret at a Freemasons' Lodge in Buckinghamshire. It was set within beautiful grounds amid scenic flowerbeds, rolling lawns and a fountain, and populated by squirrels, birds and rabbits.

It was good money, a free slap up meal, and a good networking opportunity, in exchange for just a short set of perennials like *Hi Ho Silver Lining* and *The Wild Rover*, so that the Brethren could sing along to the choruses, and bang on the tables a bit.

Unfortunately, I'd been greedy at the weekend, and worked long sets on Friday and Saturday, then doubled two jobs thirty miles apart on Sunday. I was half asleep, with a raw throat and a singing voice like cold gravel and weaker than a butter spanner.

This was a showbiz lodge, crammed with seasoned speciality acts, musos, and comics, so whereas I could've winged it to the Great British public, this lot knew the difference between a pro and a blagger, and expected a stellar performance from an equal.

I'd got the gig via a magician I'd chatted to at another show. It turned out we knew a lot of the same people in the biz. When he asked me to do a turn at this function, I did suggest he check my act out first given the calibre of the patrons, but he said he had nothing to worry about - if I worked for the names we'd both dropped, he knew they wouldn't associate with any old tat...

On the night, while everyone was on the coffee and After Eights, *"Mr. Magic"* got up and introduced me thus:
"If I can have your attention please, gents. I'm confident you'll enjoy your after dinner cabaret. I don't know this young man that well, but we got to talking at an event recently, and I'm sure from

the content of our conversations that he is very good indeed. Let's have a big round of applause for Dave Dawson!"

 I went onstage with a fraction of my powers, and did OK.. but in front of my peers, not OK enough. I went down like a granite life-belt, walking off to the sound of the wildlife outside.

 My illusionist friend then got up and returned to the boards, his footsteps hammering home the silence further still. He stood positioned on the exact spot where I had just theatrically died. Motioning over to where I had retaken my seat, he whispered:
 "Thanks David.. that was..."
 His voiced petered off to a hush, and he hung his head to eye what must have been a particularly enthralling knot in the wood below. Then he sighed, before murmuring,
 "When I was little, mummy told me... never..talk....to strangers"

❖❖❖❖

 A gentleman recovering from a triple bypass operation asked for some Country & Western. I chose *Achy Breaky Heart.*

❖❖❖❖

 I was contracted by a company shedding most of its workforce, to play what was referred to within the terms as a *"Reduncancy*

Party"*, although all the banners in the hall tried to soften the blow, calling it a *"Thank You Celebration"*
"I can turn that round", I reckoned.
Nope.

❖❖❖❖

I was booked for another post-meal cabaret. It was an awards bash for a nationwide sales team, at a swanky conference centre, and had been in the diary for months, but unfortunately now clashed with an England World Cup qualifier. The organisers assured me however that all employees were to attend on pain of losing their bonuses. There'd be furtive glances at phones to check the score during my spot, but what the hell... it'll be fine.

It was in a ginormous ballroom with a long, paid, bar, squashed tight with about three hundred top quartile reps. I was match-fit and buzzing. Nothing could go wrong...
... except the alarm bell and piped message moments before my slot, inviting "anybody interested in an alternative to the cabaret to exit the hall onto the veranda, which will feature Sky Sports..."

All the men got up with a Wembley Stadium-proportioned roar and hopped it through the patio doors, leaving just a hundred ladies. Oh well, I thought. I'll just do the "girly set" that I used to play in the hen nights. The job was still recoverable.

"...where complimentary drinks will be served", concluded the announcement, causing them to leave, too.

It was just me and the barman. I listened out for the sound of a little boy on a squeaky tricycle pedalling around the corridors, as I suddenly realised I'd become a *"Cabaret Jack Torrance"* in the main suite at The Overlook Hotel in *The Shining*.

My solitary audience member chuckled when I reached for my acoustic and *I Think I'm Alone Now, Heartbreak Hotel* and *All By Myself* all echoed around the cavernous emptiness.

"All the people.. so many people" from *Parklife*. I did that, too.

❖❖❖❖

I played every month at an East End pub frequented by many *"gentlemen of honour"*. Yes, you guessed right... that's gangsters again. Under no other circumstances imaginable would I ever have been accepted to mix with them, or persuade them to mince about in the open air as part of a human locomotive.

It was a Saturday night. *Amarillo* was high in the charts, and my voice was flying from my very guts to compete with the turmoil. The joint was creaking at the seams and literally *everybody,* including the barstaff, snaked around the lounge in a

50 foot conga line, clattering into the tables and knocking glasses flying. I programmed the next two tracks into my sound system on autoplay and yelled as loudly as I could,

  "Right Everyone!! Health and safety alert!! Beer garden!!",
and vaulted offstage, and out the back door with my radio mic, and the whole pub following. I felt like the Plaistow Pied Piper.

  As the song jumped into *The Locomotion*, then *Love Train*, we weaved onto the decking and then out further, bumping into stationary cars, staggering about as a yelping procession of "railway coaches", then back inside in unison.

  At my next gig there, one of the "carriages" turned up just as I was leaving. I said I was heading home on the A40, and loudly mentioned us all acting as daft as brushes the last time.

  In my misplaced bonhomie, however, I forgot the gangsters' unwritten Code of Conduct, invisibly stating that they can never be seen as playing the fool, as it was all about "not losing face".

  With a humourless smirk plastered across his face, he bundled me to one side with the immortal words,
  "All jokes aside, Dave, if I ever find out on the grapevine that you told anyone about me doing the hokey cokey in the car park as part of a long choo choo train, you won't be *on* the motorway.. you'll be *in* it.. anyway.. safe journey home, son"

❖❖❖❖

I did another mass sacking soirée, for the BBC. I might get spotted by a talent scout, I thought. Literally everybody stayed at the bar next door. One bloke doddered in, swigging from a bottle of wine, and I asked if he had any requests.

"Yesss. Wherezz the toiletzz...."

"Same place as my career at the moment", I said.

❖❖❖❖

Some genius at a Summer Fete pitched me three feet away from the burger barbecue on a very windy day, blowing plumes of black smog and ash all over me as I was performing.

"Oi mate!" said a passer by. "I've got a request for ya! Do *Smoke Gets In Your Eyes!*"... because obviously I hadn't thought of that.

"Nice one!", I said, literally squinting against the fumes.

"Excuse me", said the next one. "Have you got *Smoke Gets In Your Eyes*? Only I thought, what with-"

"Yeh, I get it mate", I said wiping embers from my white shirt

"You know what song you should do, don't you?", said the third

"Is it called *Unoriginal Audience Member?*", I replied

"No mate!", he said "It's *Smoke Gets-*"

"Right, I'm off" I said, and packed up.

❖❖❖❖

I played every year for five years at the annual *"Blind Bowlers' Association Awards"*, and the same players were in the audience each time. I went onstage at the last one and said,

"It's so nice to see so many familiar faces here tonight. Put your hands up if you've seen me before"

❖❖❖❖

I played at a lady's 95th birthday and went down so well that the family pencilled me in for her 96th. She survived the year, and they liked me again, and so forth. With lighter, "greyer" pencil, I handwrote each decreasingly unlikely repeat birthday into my diary. When it came to her 100th, the pencil broke as I was writing it in, which in hindsight I really should have taken as a sign. The contract, posted to me a week before the momentous occasion, stipulated that this time it was not a birthday party, but instead a *"Celebration of the Life of Edna Higgins"*.

What a quaint turn of phrase, I thought, as I'd never heard it before. I reckoned she'd also be getting a telegram from The Queen, so this was going to be an extra special one.

Come the day, the chair next to the stage, that Edna always sat in, was empty. In a childish, playful voice, I said,

"Come on now Edna, don't be shy. Come out for your party!!"

After a collective gasp from the assembled crowd, who I now suddenly noticed were all dressed in sombre black, the son rushed up and whispered in my ear what *"celebration of life"* meant in current parlance. Oh Christ.

I came home and threw away the pencil.

❖❖❖❖

I played a Country set at a Wake for a chap who'd died in his sleep, forgetting the small print on the contract stating:
 "Johnny Cash, Kenny Rogers etc.. NOT The Gambler"

The *"God, No"* moment when singing the forbidden song and realising what line followed *"and the best you can hope for…"* had me dreading that my own funeral might be next.

❖❖❖❖

I committed a similar grisly faux pas at another Remembrance bash, when I was permitted to play some 50s rock and roll to lighten the mood, and of all the classics in my repertoire I went for *That'll Be The Day…* that I die. Again… it nearly was.

Chapter 17.
The Smelly I.D. Parade

I arrived home after a Sunday 3pm-6pm club gig with a pizza. That long weekend, I'd also seen off a Thursday pub, a Friday wine bar, and a Saturday wedding. I was uncoiling nicely. I popped a tinny and was a slice into my thin-crust... when I got a breathless call from a new booker. The regular weekly singer at a South London pub an hour away had just phoned in with the flu - please could I drop everything and bail him out *pronto*.

I threw the Seafood Supreme and beer in the fridge for later and hopped straight back into the still warm motor, but not before texting my old mate Griller, a fan who used to see me perform regularly at a Shepherd's Bush community centre before it got knocked down. Actually, he was such a tough nut that he may have been in it *while* the bulldozers were smashing it to bits, walking out of the debris defiant, clutching his pint and laughing at the cracks he'd made in the demolition ball. His answerphone message summed him up:

"This is Griller's phone. I'm not here. If I don't know ya, you'd better have a bloody good reason to leave a message"

I hadn't seen him for years but remembered that he lived, or rather lurked, where I was headed. He was hard as Stonehenge and about four foot across - a larger Bob Hoskins, with a nose like a margarine anvil. He loved his crooners and always dressed impeccably, squeezed into silk suits over Italian shirts and ties, and you would not mess. I never asked what he did for work.

I got to the little pub in the nick of time. It was in a side street with fifteen people in it. I lugged the gear in, and was heralded by the hubbub grinding to a hush. That, and the usual darts in mid-air *"let's all stare at the mutant who's not from round here"* ritual synonymous with many inhospitable locals-only saloons. I think even the jukebox was in on the hostility and switched itself off. I've never grasped the malice towards a stranger all by himself who's come to try and make you happy, but it festered in this boozer this evening.. and probably all others.

"Oo' are you?", asked a gangly, rat-faced forty-something malevolently, pivoting on his stool as I set myself up in a recess.
"The cavalry", I answered cheerily. "I just drove from twenty miles away to help out... your normal guy's sick"
"You'd better be as good as Adam", he bristled
"I don't know Adam from Adam so I wouldn't know", I replied
"What do you mean you don't know Adam? Everybody knows Adam. He plays here every week!", he replied, agitated
"Well I play in Eastcote every other week", I said
"Where's that?", he asked

"Exactly", I said.

When I tuned my guitar, someone complained that I should have done that before I got there. As any stringed instrument player will confirm, this is like ordering an ice sculptor to make a swan before driving with the top down in the middle of August.

At "on your marks" I put on a brave face:-
"Right, people", I said. "I've got a thousand songs up here and tonight I am your human jukebox... just watch where you stick the money! What are we in the market for this evening?"

Absolutely no reaction.
OK, I'll make the selections then.

I was on good form; my voice, like my car, hadn't cooled down and my fingers were still dexterous from the lunchtime job. But I wasn't Adam and I was treated heinously for that crime - apathy, insults, swearing, even threats in the toilet on my break.

If things are going South at a gig, an old trick is to play very long songs, thus reducing gaps in between, invaded by bad-natured heckling, or silence. If you ever see an act go down like a Khamikhaze pilot that came back, treating the crowd to Genesis' eighteen minute *Supper's Ready,* or a non-stop Oasis medley in alphabetical order, and they're only up to *All Around The World* half an hour later, they may be brighter than you think.

I chose *American Pie*, just a few verses short of the Quran, elongated to infinity by an extended intro and four guitar solos.
 "Oi Mate!", cried a voice
 'Rat Face' had wobbled off his perch, and we were nose to snout. He reeked of pork scratchings and pale ale.
 "When is this ending, mush? ZZ Top were clean shaven when you started you started this number!"

I tried endearing myself to individual audience members. I saw an Eagles T-shirt and played *Take It Easy,* and an AC/DC badge, so played *Back in Black*. I saw a Timberland shirt and played *Knock On Wood*. I was as popular as a mobile at The Crucible.

When someone grunted for me to do some Sinatra I leapt at it. This was my speciality, so I belted out my finest *Mack The Knife*. That'll redeem me, I thought. It'll be a piece of cake now.
 "The bastard's miming", he seethed. "I might headbutt 'im"
 "I'll prove I wasn't!", I snapped, my voice tremoring in panic...
 "I won't sing *Mack The Knife*, I'll sing *Colin The Fork* or some other bloke's name over my track instead .. How's that?"
 "Go on then, Harry Cronic Junior", came the reply

So I did, not oblivious to the ridiculousness of crooning *Stan The Spoon* over my big band backing to avoid a battering.

Accepting that I was the real deal, he begrudgingly muttered:
"Flash fucker"

"Ask 'im if he does impressions", came a voice from the fruit machine. "...as if he's singing's not funny enough"

"Actually", I said ,"I could grab a tea towel from the kitchen, take my tie off and knot it around my head, and sing *This Ole House* and *Green Door* if you like. I'd be *Sheik*in' Stevens"
I even desperately tried resorting to self-deprecation.
"I nearly got lost on the way here.. but you weren't that lucky"
"Do you like good music? Yes? What are you doing here then?"
"Here's a beautiful song..Well, it *was*. Then *I* got hold of it"

After a none too shabby *He Aint Heavy*... I heard:
"You aint a patch on Adam, why don't you go 'ome?"
"I'm staying out of spite", I replied
"Adam with flu is better than you. Just eff off... you're rubbish"
"Rubbish?! Er, did you hear my last song?"
"I sincerely hope so!", he scoffed.

I finished at 11pm and someone tapped their watch and said,
"Hold up, where do you think you're skiving off to? Adam always goes on till half eleven!"

"I'll tell you what then, shall I!" I said, switching the mains off, now thoroughly pee'd off. "Why not shoot round his house, drag him out of his sickbed, dose him up with Lemsip and carry him down here.. he can do your last half hour"

As I curled the leads up, a nice woman asked for a card, saying to take no notice of this lot as she'd loved my work. She worked for a blue chip company. I'd be ideal for some of their corporate work. Would I go as far as Kensington?

"Madam...", I said "...tonight I'd travel to Jupiter, just to escape this petri dish of plankton". She left happy.

I then heard someone mumble loud enough for me to hear:

"He won't be coming back here again"

I didn't stop dismantling but just replied:

"That's completely unacceptable and won't stand up in court... verbally just isn't good enough.. he wants it in writing"

I was all packed up and about to depart sharpish, when the pub door slammed open and I heard:

"*DAVEY BOY!! GOT YOUR MESSAGE FELLA!!*",

...and looked up to see my old friend, Griller, with his arms stretched so wide the buttons at his midriff nearly pinged off his Armani. Harold Shand as Jesus on an invisible cross.

"Fancy looking up old Griller after all this time!", he laughed, clenching me in such a tight bear hug that I nearly choked up an anchovy from my aborted dinner. He let go and asked,

"Good gig?"

"Don't", I sighed. "I went down crap, depping for someone that plays here every week. All the twats here have got a thing for their Adam. I think they've all got steamy pics of him on their bedroom walls and they're going home now to have a little fiddle. I should have sang *My Adam Is A Centrefold*"

This insult could have resulted in a thrashing just two minutes earlier, but the odds had now shortened… a dozen or so spineless bastards against a very hacked-off singer and twenty horsepower in a suit. It now just elicited nervous trembling along the bar.

"You aint finished are ya, Davey?", asked Griller. "I've come all this way! Well, actually only about four doors down but that's by the by. Gissa song Davey… be like the old days at the club, go on"

I was shagged out. I looked at my gear, stacked in a pile, ready to go, then at his *"please"* face, and back at that heavy rig that I'd already put up and pulled down twice today, for two gigs.

"Heaven forbid I make it big, Griller" I said. "You can tell all and sundry about the time I almost gave myself a hernia just to knock you out a private *Summer Wind*"

"Good boy", he smiled

I built the whole kit back up, sang his song, and then brought it all back down again.

"Let's get a drink fella.. what'll it be?", he cackled

"Do I need one", I sighed

He pulled out his silver money clip. It was empty. He stared at it sourly, then tugged all his pocket linings inside out, and beat along his chest, now looking like a bespoke King Kong.

"I've only forgotten me readies, David", he said, not without shame. "I appear to have financially embarrassed myself"

Then his face dawned into a smile, and he stuck up his finger, as big as a sausage, in an *"all is not lost"* way, slowly scanning it around the whole pub... a sinister, sweeping second hand ticking on a wound-up watch. The place went deathly quiet.

"By way of recompense Mr. Dawson...", he said, "...and because I never like to let down an old friend.. I would like you to take a good look around this dive and point out to me which one of these no-marks has given you the hardest time tonight"

I moved my eyes gradually along an I.D. parade of perspiring, fidgeting cowards, all smelling of fear, biting their lips and staring with intense terror at their cigarette packets and pints.

Oh Sweet Lord, the Temptation.

Chapter 18.
Divine Comedies

Sometimes, The Cosmos deigns to sprinkle fairy dust over a gig, annointing it at a crucial moment so that whatever the act may do to louse it up just has the opposite effect...

...like the time my minidisc player died and I stupidly hadn't brought my spare. I bungled through on my acoustic, brazenly taking on songs I didn't know, that all fell apart quicker than a cobweb staircase. It was all going dreadfully, until every fuse in the place blew, plunging the pub into pitch blackness. Every fuse, that is, except for the electrics running my amp.

I was singing *There Is A Light That Never Goes Out* at the time, and valiantly played on in the dark, following with *I Can See Clearly Now,* and, of course, *Dancing In The Dark.* By the time the power was eventually restored, I'd been reprieved.

❖❖❖❖

I was ill-prepared at a cabaret job when someone shouted for a number needing a capo. For the uninitiated, that's the guitar clamp so that we can play open chords higher up the neck. I usually kept it by my mixer but I'd been careless and forgotten.

It was in my cable bag, a tatty old Lidl carrier, tucked away unseen behind the stage curtains. I dragged it out under full view of the spotlights, rooting around inside. The whole crowd spotted it, with one bloke good-naturedly shouting:

"Bloody hell Dave! On the money *you're* earning you can't afford to shop somewhere a bit more upmarket you tight git?"

I suddenly noticed that the gear had been "double-bagged". The original must have perished or split so I'd pulled another one around it to stop everything falling out.

"Oh, please let it be", I thought to myself, stripping the Lidl layer away... and it was. I strutted to the lip of the stage with my prize held aloft, like an executioner proudly displaying the severed head after a guillotining. Rather than talk and risk sullying the glory of the moment with a weak one-liner, I put on the stoniest face I could muster, and stayed silent.

It was a ravaged Waitrose bag, ripped to ribbons and riddled with holes. The place went doolally.

..and the funniest part, for me at least... the Lidl bag was obviously of a much better quality!

❖❖❖❖

I'd just butchered Queen's *We Are The Champions* at a club, starting on guitar in the wrong key and hoping I could bluff it. It was fine until I got to the high notes. I was the dog at Crufts that sees the hurdle and runs around the side at the last second.

A voice from the crowd justifiably called out:
"If Freddie Mercury was to walk in now he'd have your guts!"
"Well, he's not likely to, is he??" I shouted back, cockily…"What with him first and foremost still being *dead*, and all!!"

At that precise second a bloke strolled in the door. He had the same slightly bucked teeth, an identical moustache and hair, and even wore pale blue jeans similar to those that Freddie wore at *Live Aid*. He resembled one of those *AI* pictures of how rock stars would have looked today had they lived.

To his bemusement but obvious delight, the whole place roared with laughter, and applauded his perfectly-timed entrance. It really was *A Kind of Magic* digging me out of a hole.

"Bloody hell" I said, gesturing towards him. "He's made a full recovery! The *Show Must Go On* though! Sorry Freddie!!"

❖❖❖❖

It was a Sports Bar frequented by rockers. I get by as a guitar player, so *Alright Now*, *Sweet Home Alabama*, *Layla* and songs in that vein usually fit the bill... but I'd just bought a white Fender Stratocaster similar to the iconic model favoured by Jimi Hendrix. A punter spotted the connection and said,

"You've got the Hendrix guitar. Play us some Jimi"

"No problem", I said. "Here's *Hey Joe*"

"Ah, you're not getting away that easy", he replied. "Play *All Along The Watchtower*. Go on... I dare you"

He was canny, this one. To an intermediary player like myself, *Hey Joe* was a walk in park. *All Along The Watchtower*, on the other hand, was a walk in the car wash.

I have a monologue I often wheel out before arduous requests. I say that *90%* had been knocked off the price of my guitar by the shop, because it was part of a bad batch off the production line - the wiring had been cocked up, so when it was plugged in, the wrong notes would sometimes come out of it. If that happened during the next song, I'd give the audience the phone number of the factory to complain to, as it was nowt to do with me.

It didn't bail me out though. I blundered through the number, longing for its demise as much as the scowling spectators. It was met with stunned consternation and a single, sublime heckle:

"More like *All Along The Botchtower!!*"

"Well", I said, carefully placing my abused Stratocaster back on its stand. "I'm sure that Mr Hendrix would've agreed that to be a *radical* departure from the original. Luckily for him, he wasn't here to *Experience* it or voice his opinion. Sadly, we were"

The gig was nearly unsalvagable... or it would have been... for as soon as I finished speaking, the guitar fell sideways off the stand of its own accord, with a loud clang and a wail of feedback.

"Ah", I said, without missing a beat, looking up to the Heavens with my hands clasped in prayer. "Perhaps he *did* hear it after all! The Maestro has spoken. Thanks for the review, Jimi"

The crowd howled, and I thanked providence for granting me *"some kind of way outta there"*, with my reputation intact.

❖❖❖❖

In my early days, I was badgered into singing *The House Of The Rising Sun* at a club next to a fire station. Despite protesting that I couldn't compete with Eric Burdon's rendition, I finally buckled under the pressure. It was a rookie mistake.

I'm far too long in the game to fall for this old chestnut now. Like Elvis' *American Trilogy*, or Pavarotti's *Nessun Dorma*, this song is one hell of a tall order, and some more vindictive patrons, particularly in social clubs, demand it not because they want to hear that you *can* do it, but because they want to hear that you *can't*. They can then bring you down a peg and moan to their mates that the artist *"isn't up to much"* because they can't sing *everything*. The more ridiculous the request, the better.

This is, of course, completely absurd. At the lowest level of the entertainment industry, where the rewards are smallest, the pressures are highest. It's impossible for even an all-rounder to be fantastic at *everything*. Nevertheless, the impossible is not only expected but *demanded*, and we're exposed to flak if we fall short. At the other end of the spectrum, where millions are to be made, you'd never dream of reading a review stating:

"Madonna's woeful performance at the Superdome last night left fans incensed. Although her pop hits were very good, as they ruddy well should be, she didn't do any Irish rebel songs, Knees Up Mother Brown Singalongs, grime, or Bon Jovi, and only played for a measly three hours, snubbing demands to carry on even when they offered to pass the hat round for £17.26 in loose change for another hour. Fans were left stunned when she played a guitar and wasn't better than the bloke from Van Halen, while some took to social media complaining that by refusing to encore with 'Der Hölle Rache' in Dm from Mozart's 'The Magic Flute', she was admitting she was rubbish. To top it all, during a pitch-perfect version of her breakthrough hit,

"Holiday", she was called a big head for objecting to a pissed teenager storming the stage, pushing a phone up to her ear and shouting in her face to get this shit off and sing this Nicki Minaj song or actually let HER do it because she was miles better than Madonna. Many demanded refunds"

...that's a fair assessment of what we all have to put up with.

Anyway, I foolishly gave the song a go, downtuning my guitar by half a step to give myself a fighting chance, but still mauled it. It ended to jeers and another clever put down, this time:
 "*House Of The Rising DAMP,* more like"

On the ropes, I declared this an opportune time to take my break, and at that moment a fire engine trundled out from next-door with sirens blaring, sounding just like a police car.

 "Yes, I'm sorry I just killed The Animals officers!!", I shouted over the mic. "I'm guessing the R.S.P.C.A. must have reported me?!! It *was* a first offence!! OK.. I'll come quietly"

I interlocked my hands, then put them behind my head with my elbows out, and left the club, to the sound of the still wailing sirens. Once outside, judging from the laughter echoing inside, I knew The Universe had pulled another win out of the Lidl bag.

Chapter 19.
"Tickets available At The bra"

I once saw a typo on a club poster that made me think of exorcists and priests crossing themselves, throwing Holy Water onto the stage everywhere, and intoning grave incantations in a bid to rid themselves of a recent live music abomination. It read:

"*Dave Dawson's performance is soon to be repented*"

❖❖❖❖

I also *"fell fowl"* of careless punctuation, and spacing, when advertised on a flyer for an Ex-Servicemen's Dinner & Dance, which proclaimed, in a florid, flowery font:

"*Dave Dawson sings Frank Sinatra, Dean Martin, Nat King Cole and Chicken Casserole*"...

...and the Chinese Restaurant which I imagined being descended upon by Hannibal Lecter and other assorted cannibals, eager to tuck in, attracted by the advert in the local paper:

"*Buffet and Dave Dawson. Eat as much as you like*"

❖❖❖❖

I envisaged cowering under a barrage of tiny Dutch Tungsten arrows as part of the competition, with most of them hitting the mark, and emerging punctured and bloodied. A team of professionals over from Holland for the World Championships were making a diversion to a pub in Kent on the way, for an Exhibition Match. The hoarding outside read:

"*Darts Tournament plus Dave Dawson. Do not miss*"

❖❖❖❖

As morbid as it was, I wept with laughter at this Working Men's Club poster, and the Hammer Horror imagery of the coffin lid being prised off in the lounge after the prize draw:

"*A Memorial Service will be held for our much loved member Bert Ryan, followed by a raffle and "Open The Box""...*

...and the beautifully skewed concept of *The King* materialising from the Hereafter and releasing new material that wasn't as good as the stuff recorded up until his demise in 1977:

"*Come and see Steve Collins as Elvis Presley, singing all of his best songs from before he died. Book early*" ...

...Or the British Legion brochure which read:

"*Mickey Thomas returns as Tommy Cooper*", and the glorious disclaimer in small print at the bottom of the poster. I quote:

"*Following complaints from members at a previous show, we would like to make it clear that this is a tribute act and not the real Tommy Cooper, who sadly passed away onstage in 1984*"

Chapter 20.
"A cold front down South"

Following a rollicking set at a Trades Club, a couple asked if I'd be willing to play at their luxury retreat. It's easy to get blasé after a great show, and my immediate acceptance without any cursory questions filled them with such glee that I wondered if I wasn't exposing myself to something untoward.

Sensing my apprehension, they reassured me with their official website. It boasted effusive testimonials and glossy photos of sprawling grounds, a swish spa, casino, à la carte restaurant, and cabaret suite. Impressed at both the venue and the fee - £200 for 45 minutes - I agreed to appear. I was also pleasantly surprised at the informality of the complex. There wasn't even a dress code.

They were so unfeasibly delighted that I did some Googling when I got home and very soon "uncovered" why they were so thrilled. I would have been "exposing myself", alright... it was a nudist resort. Although I wasn't allowed to wear any of my own, I did have appropriate material, as my repertoire included *I Who Have Nothing, Little Things Mean A Lot, Blowing In The Wind* and *I've Got A Lovely Bunch of Coconuts.*

I said I couldn't do the date because sadly "I had something on".

Chapter 21.
"In Da (Social) Club"

I played a club near Heathrow, dying so badly that there should have been a chalk outline of myself on the floor and a forensics team draping *"Police - Do Not Cross"* tape around the stage area.

It was a ball ache from the off. Within spitting distance of the stage door were *five* empty bays, but I was haughtily informed that these were for committee members only, so I had to park so far away I was halfway home again.

Then, as I carted my heavy speakers in, I asked a drinker to just shift his stool a weeny bit so I could get past.
"Who do you think you are, Lionel Fucking Richie??", he asked. "Go around and use the other door, ya twat"

The audience were both disinterested and downright abusive. Gauging the average age to be dead or older, I knew I'd get grief over the volume. Before I even plugged in, I asked myself out loud which guitar I should use, and a creaky voice at a nearby table playing pontoon croaked *"the quiet one"*. I was determined to deny this shower of sods the satisfaction of a complaint.

I set my sound so low I could barely hear it, and cracked into a scarcely discernible *That's Life* that was in danger of being drowned out by the air-conditioning. Sure enough, a Jurassic old duffer at the card table, with a grey blazer and matching face, outstretched his tweed arm horizontally, moving it up and down with the palm inverted, in the universal, very discourteous sign for *"Turn It Down"*. He was six inches away from my speaker, so presumably couldn't hear his Jack of Clubs hitting the table. I was having none of it. I stopped the song, and asked:

"What's with bouncing the invisible basketball? Do you play invisible badminton too? When did they let you out the asylum?"

In response to my confrontational opening banter, a wide-eyed woman behind the bar waved her arms manically above her head. I instantly guessed I was ribbing someone integral to being booked at this manky hut, and should stop this outrageous verbal assault immediately, but continued digging my own hole, just for my own amusement. What did it matter? I already had no intention of playing this belligerent khazi again. I addressed the lady directly, and the whole place turned their attention towards her flaying limbs and vigorously shaking head.

"I see we've got Air Traffic Control's manual division in as well! Who knew Terminal Five stretched this far out?! Did you forget your flags? Is that why you're just waving your arms about?"

She became even more frenetic, desperately and wordlessly mouthing a very wide, very loud but silent *"NO NO NO"*.

"It's no good saying *"NO"* madam!" I said, straightfaced. "Tell it to the pilot of the seven four seven you're directing down onto the roof as we speak! There are lives at stake woman!"

An old crone who was a deadringer for a Toby Jug, and just as motionless, clenched her face and growled:

"He's on the committee and he's telling you you're too loud, and you are. Now turn it bloody down!"

"Of course it's too loud!" I said, "You're sitting right in front of my speaker cab. Didn't you do physics at school? If you want the sound to dissipate *MOVE TO THE BACK!*"

She slammed her G&T down on the table and snarled:

"I've been sitting in this seat for the past forty years!!"

"Well it's about time you stretched your legs then, isn't it!!"

I'd been onstage for one minute, sung just half a verse, chided the bar staff, and insulted two pensioners. I was as welcome as a wasp at a picnic, and the silence was broken only by the cooling system and the one-armed bandit. You may think my conduct was amateurish, and a professional would have weathered the storm, pulling the calamity back from the precipice. I probably could have done, but just couldn't be bothered... and this wasn't a gig. It was cabaret combat, pure and simple.

"I'll have you know I've played at The London Palladium!", I said, mockingly. "Admittedly I was moved on after five minutes for causing an obstruction on the pavement, but I was there!"

"The only way *you* could play The London Palladium is if you were busking outside!", someone guffawed at themselves.

"I just said that, mate." I replied "That's *literally* the punchline. You a bit slow? Do you have to run your finger under the words and say them out loud when you're reading Ladybird books?"

I was closer by the minute to pushing my nose past the 11pm finishing post, spurred on knowing I'd leave with a wedge of this ghastly shed's beer takings. A bad audience hates an act it can't break, and that's fine by me, for, to paraphase Nietzsche:

"What does not kill me makes me wonga"

"You're rubbish!", squawked a voice near the cigarette machine.

"Have some pity, then", I replied. "You've only had to put up with me for three hours. I have to listen to this crap most days!"

"Every song you've done is shit!!", yelled another

"Well at least I'm consistent!" I replied

"I'm off", said an old soak, unplumbing himself from feeding his annuity into the *Deal Or No Deal* game and tottering away.

"Oh I'm sorry Sir", I said. Was it something I sung?"

At the zenith of this skirmish interspersed with songs, two gents went to the gents. Standing at the urinal, and in full flow, so to speak, one turned to the other and said,

"That entertainer fucking *loves* himself, don't he?"

"So do I", said the other. "He's my fucking son"

The first guy bolted out of the toilets, then the club, then the town, faster than my guitar fingers noodling away behind him. He was apparently still *"half full"* when he left, with a groin area a darker shade of blue than the rest of his Wranglers.

I saw his jacket still hanging over the back of that barstool he wouldn't move a weeny bit, as we loaded the gear out. Perhaps he went home to roll himself in a big ball and die.

❖❖❖❖

"Suitable background music to be played in the break", read the "Special Conditions" of the social club contract, so I recorded a continuous *"Best of the Sixties"* compilation, to fit the bill. As it was over an hour long, I turned the external speaker off on my computer, and just let it run through to the end. Job done.

Sadly, because I'm tight, I forgot I'd gone for a free subscription with Spotify, which included adverts, and during *Sweets For My Sweet,* an old lady tripped up on the dancefloor where some numpty had spilt a drink, and fell with a thud.

As she lay writhing on the floor, the song faded out and a jingle came on with a cheery, crisp voice saying:

"Have you had an accident that's not your fault? Call *Injury Lawyers For You,* on oh eight hundred, three four-"

"SOMBODY GET A PEN! SOMEBODY GET A PEN!!", she yelled, still splayed horizontally and holding her back in pain, as the commercial led back into the 60s album... *Glad All Over.*

❖ ❖ ❖ ❖

"You've dressed up smart, young David. First impressions are so important. Well done", said the compere. It was only my fifth gig and my first for a big agent. I was keen to please.

"I'll announce you in two minutes, and you'll be coming up the steps stage left... Don't be shy, lad. Walk on with your head high"
"Rightio", I said " I won't let you down. They won't forget me."

I found out later that the agent, Del, had told the club I was only just on the circuit, and for them to put me at ease.

The butterflies flapped furiously in my stomach as the tannoy introduction filled the hall, but I took the compere's advice and lifted my chin up, pasted a smile over my face...
"And now, a new act! Please welcome Dave Dawson!!"
... and jogged up the wrong steps, through the door, and straight

into the corridor leading to the staff toilets, with the words, "Dave Dawson! *Where's* Dave Dawson!!", ringing in my ears.

I was dead right. They didn't forget me.

❖❖❖❖

I was having a corker of a Saturday night at a Snooker Social Club. The packed crowd were "having it large" to the strains of my 80s set, and I was bounding around the stage like a lunatic.

I was so shattered in my break that I took a breather outside. My interval music was playing and I started singing along to Duran Duran's *Girls On Film*, to gauge the *"phone bars"* left on my voice, and how much more high tempo material it could withstand before finally draining to empty.

A guy, hearing me, broke off from chatting to his pals and said,
  "Hold on! You aint 'arf bad, geeza.. you wanna get up there. You're better than that fucking tosser they've got on tonight"
  "What, you mean the guy singing right at this very minute?"
  "Yeh..listen to 'im! He's tragic.." he replied, hooking a thumb towards my sound sytem and screwing his face up in mock pain.
  "'ave a look at 'im too... right flashy c***, prancing about like he's at Hammersmith flamin' Odeon. Go and give him what for!"
  I'd just given 110%. I was on-form, drenched in sweat, and

panting from the exertion of geeing up two hundred revellers, all singing themselves hoarse and happily cavorting about, making the club bob on its own foundations...

...And I was *still* being slagged off.

"Do you like Duran Duran, then?", I asked him, levelly

"Yeh, Love 'em' I know their *Rio* CD backwards"

"Well, try listening to it forwards" I said. "that's Simon Le Bon singing right now. That's the CD. *I'm* the fucking tosser"

❖❖❖❖

The drummer is almost always the last member of the band to leave a gig, because of the amount of kit they have to pack away. A friend was all alone unscrewing his cymbals when he spotted someone fifty yards away giving him hateful looks from the bar. The guy put his pint of bitter down, walked over, and said,

"Your band was shit"

"We're fooling a lot of people then. We gig every weekend"

"Still shit"

"Were you born or hatched? You sound like a little cock"

"Do you want to discuss this outside??", shouted the cretin

Just then, the rest of the band came back from a cigarette break. "Absolutely", said the drummer without missing a beat "...but I don't do solo work, we only go out as a four piece"

❖❖❖❖

For many years, I worked with an agent who'd started out as an act. He played the circuit for decades before retreating to the safety of his Slough bunker to send troops such as I into the fray, rather than go out himself. After half a lifetime of performing, he had no intention of strapping on a guitar again.

His wife was also tired of a quarter century's lonely weekends. She far preferred him collecting a humble 15% of other acts' fees, as they sang and he sofa'd. And, of course, a thriving agency with a roster of quality acts only needs a dozen onstage on the same night to exceed what he would have earned himself.

I have a lot of time for agents that used to be acts. They remind me of "Madams" in brothels because they never put us in a situation where they haven't already been shafted themselves.

Anyway, this agent, Ray, was in a tight spot one night. Just as he was tucking into his dinner, the male guitar/vocalist he'd booked into a local club phoned. He'd broken down on the way and it was only an hour before show time.

There was no chance at all of Ray finding a replacement at such a late hour, so he didn't even bother trying. He just bit the bullet, like a grizzled old sheriff forced out of retirement just one more time to save the town... or in this case, his reputation and all future bookings with this regular venue.

Ray dusted off his shotgun (*OK, the Gibson*), heaved his P.A. system from the courthouse (*OK, his airing cupboard*), mounted his steelhorse (*OK, got in an Audi*), and cranked up A *Fistful of Dollars* on his stereo (*OK, Radio 5 Live - he WAS pushing fifty*). Then he headed out to do his first gig for about ten years.

Luckily for Ray, he'd done all of his business remotely with this club via phone and email, and had never set foot in there. Just as fortuitously, the poor act on the hard shoulder of the M4 would have been making his debut there, and hadn't sent posters or photos... so nobody knew what either of them looked like. Ray was therefore able to breeze in and and pass himself off as his featured artist, with nobody any the wiser.

He says he fumbled through the job and got by, but I have it on good authority that in his day he was one of the best on the circuit. Even allowing for cobwebs, his "fumbled through" would be most other acts' "absolute barnstormer".

It was near to midnight by the time he'd loaded the car up, but rather than be allowed to collect his fee and head for home, he was summoned for an after hours' drink by the Club Secretary. This is like being kept back for detention by an avuncular head master, which doesn't end until he's given you your money... and whereas he probably lives only a short walk away, you've got a twenty mile, one hour drive ahead of you.

The secretary sat him down, and with just the two of them left in the building, Ray had to endure war stories about fledgling acts such as Cannon and Ball and Alvin Stardust playing early shows at the club and going down like a copper kite... as well as industrial strength praise about himself.

He knocked back his warm bottle of bitter, with an increasing sense of foreboding. The guy gushed that Ray was the best act they'd had there in years. He'd be straight onto the agent in the morning, to get him back every last Friday of the month for the next thirty years or until they all died, whichever came soonest.

This was bad news for Ray, who by now realised he'd screwed himself over by playing a bit too well... which he'd *had* to do, or be reprimanded for palming them off with a duff act.

The whole charade was destined to end in tears.

At best, he'd be back gigging once a month, having left life on the road behind, with his wife sitting home alone again. If his reputation spread, which was on the cards, he could be cajoled into playing even *more* gigs. On top of running the agency, he'd be overstretched, just when he was trying to wind things down.

At worst, it would inevitably come out that Ray and his "new act" were one and the same. The club would then think he couldn't be trusted. And that would mean a dishonest agent was operating in the entertainment industry, which would lead to its immediate collapse. I'm of course being deadly serious.

Ray drained his half and tried to make good his escape, but his host insisted he have another with him, and continued to froth on about their glorious future together.

Then he had to have another. And a fourth. He finally managed to extricate his money and himself from his new best mate's clutches and enthusings at about 1am, no doubt relishing the impending *"welcome home, finally"* lecture from his missus.

Bracing himself for awful news, Ray phoned the club at 11am the next day for feedback on how "his act" had been received on his debut. His new pal, the Entertainment Secretary, answered.

"Er yes, it's Ray here, your agent", he said, hoping his voice wouldn't be recognised. "I was just checking in on how my new artist went down at the club last night?"

"He was shit and at the end we couldn't bloody well get rid of him. Don't ever send him back", came the response...
...an argument which, as we know from what happened in reality, held less water than a candy floss bucket.
Phew! That was close!

It was, at last, first-hand confirmation for Ray of a suspicion he'd held for years… The client's version of events will be as far from the artist's - and, therefore, the truth - as a CEO's Self Assessment Tax Return (allegedly, of course).

❖❖❖❖

Someone shouted out asking if I did anything by The Who.
"*I Can't Explain*!" I said.
"Well it's a simple enough bloody question!", replied the fan.

❖❖❖❖

A homophobic moron who'd just professed his dislike for gay men, shouted for something he could dance to, so I played *Young Hearts Run Free* and mentally wet myself watching him get up and throw some shapes to me singing about *"my man and me"*.

❖❖❖❖

I had a club in Acton where a bloke always turned up near the end, selling seafood out of a basket. Sometimes I'd sing *Prawn To Be Wild*, *Wishing Whelk*, *Pictures of Crabstick Men*, or, of course, *Pulling Mussels From a Shell* when he arrived, much to the amusement of, well, just me. I saw him swoop in once, put the hamper down, and, with his back to me, ferret around for some jellied eels or winkles for a hungry customer.

"Right! Here's lunch everyone!!", I shouted... only to see a very shocked young lady jolting round and looking at me aghast, as she pulled her baby out of a Mothercare bassinet carrier.

❖❖❖❖

I'd just done a Sunday night at a grimy club in Bedfordshire. It was my fifth job of the week, and I was running on fumes. A great part of being a solo is the rush you get walking out of a show, knowing you've done it all by yourself, but I was still knackered, and soon seriously doubting my sanity.

I lugged my first big speaker out and returned for the other. It wasn't there. I was so frazzled that I thought I must have already loaded it. I checked the car... nothing. I feared I was going mad, as I hurried around every room in the club. It was nowhere to be seen. Eventually, reluctantly, I left for home. I'll never forget that midnight journey back on the M25, ironically steering into a large curve, whilst panicking that the amount of work I was taking on might well be driving me round the bend.

A *terrible* part of being a solo is that each trip to the car leaves the rest of the gear unattended, just asking to be stolen. The club had "apparently" seen nothing, so I went to the police, who got hold of the venue's VHS recordings. It *had* been pinched, but I was quite relieved not to have taken leave of my senses.

Sure enough, the footage showed some toe-rag in grainy black and white time delay frames, staggering under the weight of the big black cab and plonking it in the back of a big black cab... which then drove off, headed for who knew where.

The police arrested a club member who was a ringer for the "perp" on film. They repeatedly asked him if he was the same man as on the video, and he kept on exercising his right to "*no comment*". Finally, one of the interrogating officers said:
"For the benefit of the tape, you'll observe the man on the video is wearing a black jumper. Do you have a jumper like that?"

In a prime example of the mouth letting the clutch out before the brain has changed gear, he replied,
"I did have, but I burnt it"
Suffice to say, his career as a criminal mastermind ended that day. A nicked speaker literally led to a "nicked speaker".

❖❖❖❖

I played a private gig and was touched to observe a lit-up sign proudly embossed with the word *"SINGER"*, onstage, indicating precisely where I was to stand, whilst simultaneously informing the attendees of my role in the evening's proceedings...
...Only later did I realise I was playing at the *"Singer Car and Sewing Machine Owners' Annual Dinner"*.

❖❖❖❖

I played a rugby team's social club with a stinking cold. It was my sixth long gig in five days, and I didn't even have the energy reserves to use my stagecraft to save the day. I made a total pig's ear of it and went down like a vaseline doormat.

As I made a glum exit, the booker, a jolly Rastafarian, ran up with a gaping smile that engulfed his whole face, and produced a massive wodge of twenties. He eagerly peeled off my fee, plus forty smackers on top, and pressed it into my hand.
"Man, that was *fantastic!*" he said. "Here, have a drink!!"

Then he doled out another crisp note and piled it onto the rest.

"It's really good of you mate", I said. "But I was pretty shit!"
"I know man... you were *soooo* shit, they HATED YOU!"

Yes... I was confused too. At a recent AGM, half the members voted to get the place kitted out for in-house discos on Saturdays, while the other half still wanted live music. They agreed to give the latter one more try, and had a straw poll whilst I was onstage mutilating songs far safer staying on vinyl. The disco half won by a landslide. I'd totally swung it for them, albeit unwittingly.

"And in the long run, we're saving a fortune in bookings!", he laughed, thrusting yet another twenty pounds on me, as a retirement present... because neither I, nor any other singer or band, would ever play there live again. You're welcome.

❖❖❖❖

I used to play a club twice a year that had been run for decades by a straight talking Yorkshireman. After a lifetime at the sharp end, he'd now taken a back-seat to let his daughter run the entertainment, and I fancied her, although I never told her.

We chatted over a beer after one gig while settling up my fee. It was just us left - like Ray with the "headmaster" but a whole lot better. I dragged out our drink for as long as I could, but it was late and unfair to keep her, and I had the long road home.

"So I'll not see you for six months then?", I said, with a mental sniffle, as I drained my glass.

"Oh, you'll live", she laughed

I left and she locked up, but I was in such a tizz that I forgot my acoustic guitar. I was in the car, about to set off, when the porch light switched back on and the door flew open.

"Dave! You forgot your guitar! Careless!"

"No 'e 'isn't", came a gruff Yorkshire voice from inside, that, unknown to me, had been there all along...

..."He knows exactly what 'e's bloody well doing"

Chapter 22.
"Mr. Botham"

I played a British Legion with a giant lump of a DJ who was so intimidating that most people were too scared to make requests. Those who did were glared at in outrage or swatted away. He just played what the hell he wanted, to an empty floor. If he'd been a Catholic priest he'd have sat alone in the confessional all day.

Perhaps unsurprisingly, there was a dispute over his fee at the end, when all the punters, who hadn't had a dance all night, were no doubt gratefully homeward bound.

He was at loggerheads with the head barman and two of his largest staff, presumably called in as reinforcements against this disgruntled, growling man-mountain, who insisted they'd given him £100 shy of the agreed figure, and were pulling a fast one.

They weren't playing ball, and although it pains me to side with this oaf, I think they *were* trying to fob him off with a fee way below standard rates, even for a rotten job. Talks lurched to a stalemate, with neither side giving an inch.

"Last chance", he said. "Will you give me the rest of it or not?"

"No!", the trio replied in unison

"So be it" he sighed. "It's customary in such cases of deadlock for me to consort with my business partner *Mr Botham*"

Nobody had the faintest idea what he meant, but it sounded ominous. He walked exitwards, turned back, and scanned the neat row of Scotches on optics at the back of the bar, like a minesweeper, perhaps considering a wee dram for the road.

Then he left, leaving us looking at each other, speechless... but he very soon returned with "*Mr. Botham*".

Ignoring our sharp intakes of breath, he strolled briskly to the edge of the bar, then behind it, whistling a melody that was familiar but I couldn't quite place. It wasn't recited merrily, sounding gloomy and sinister. Then he gripped his "associate" with both hands, rotored "him" in a swift propellor motion above his head, and disintegrated the upturned bottle of Vintage Malt to the farthest left, with an almighty and sickening *thwack*.

As he idly drummed the ponderous cricket bat against his heel, the penny dropped. I flinched. The tune was *Ten Green Bottles*.

"That's gotta be a hundred quid down the drain for starters", he said. "Mr. Botham likes to make a strong opening statement"
"Look, there's no need for this!!", shouted the manager, as his back-up crew looked on, startled.
"Absolutely agree", said *Mr Botham's* handler. "Just settle

the outstanding and we'll be on our way"

"Thing is...", yelled the manager, "we're all cashed up and the money's away in the safe and it's on a timelock, so-"

SMASH!!! The next bottle in exploded.

"We could write you a cheque!!" he half squealed in despair.

"*...hanging on the wall. Seven green bottles...*", the DJ was singing now, as he obliterated the *THIRD* whiskey bottle.

By now, £300 was reduced to valueless ponds of sticky golden fluid and dangerous shards of broken glass on the club floor. He stood with the bat pointing to the ceiling parallel with his ear, poised for strike four, like a deranged caveman.

As for the alleged shortfall, I don't know how they got it, but they got it. Where there's a wield, there's a way....

The moral appeared to be that if a club tries to short-change you, you can fight them in the Small Claims Court, with all the red tape, time and paperwork this entails...

... or just be a sociopathic Goliath with a big bit of wood.

As it wasn't far away, I wondered if he'd borrowed it from that bloke waiting for Angus after the hen night...

"I hate to do this to you, but...."
Reasons why pubs cancel acts on the day

The toilets are flooded ☐

We're in the middle of a refurb ☐

My aunt died ☐

There's a big match on ☐

The electrics are being rewired ☐

There's another band on up the road ☐

It's not in the diary ☐

The noise people have been on ☐

We've double-booked ☐

My aunt's flooded ☐

The diary's being rewired ☐

My head barman has phoned in sick ☐

My aunt's in the middle of a refurb ☐

The electrics have phoned in sick ☐

My aunt's being rewired ☐

The noise people have flooded the toilets ☐

Chapter 23.
"Never offstage"

I'm often asked how I remember all the song lyrics, and there's no easy way. It's just constant repeat listening, usually in the car, until they stick in the mental hard drive.

I now have 4,000 downloaded inside my skull. If I memorise a number, perform it hundreds of times and then stop, I can access it decades later, word for word, chord for chord... but if I only perform it ten times, I've forgotten most of it within a year.

I also play the instrumental backing track with no vocals when driving, as a dry run for singing the song live. Almost always, I think or mouth the lines, but sometimes I sing at full pelt with the windows up, to "roadtest" whether I can hit all the notes.

I was once late for a glitzy cabaret gig, so to save time, dressed in my full stage gear at home rather than change when I got there. After all, who was ever to know?

Stopping at traffic lights, I spotted a couple in an open-topped car in the next lane, staring at me and stifling huge laughter. I soon realised they were rupturing themselves at the sight of this complete oddball in the adjacent Honda, resplendently dressed in a glittery sky blue jacket and gold "bacofoil" lamé shirt, perhaps on his way out to collect two cod and chips.

Keel had taught me an operatic trick used at open air concerts, which unleashes a voice at several decibels above what should be humanly possible, to carry across a big park. As they suppressed their cackles, I pretended not to notice, staring straight ahead. Then I selected an appropriate track without vocals, turned my stereo up on full, and pressed the button to unwind my window.

Everso, *ever so* gradually, I jerked my head to the right in tiny clicks, like a garishly dressed Las Vegas robot, until my dead eyes locked onto theirs, and then let loose with my voice, using Keel's technique over the earsplitting music, roaring:

"IT'S SUCH A PERFECT DAY.. I'M GLAD I SPENT IT WITH YOUUUUUU!"...

...and then just as slowly clicked my head back again.

This didn't *"keep them hanging on"*...
...They screeched off before the lights turned green.

I sincerely hope they didn't have a crash, as the insurance claim form could have had them sectioned.

Chapter 24.
"Stagecraft"

As I hope came across at "another club in Kent", having a decent voice is just one component of a successful act. On that particular night, mine was gritty, but I still had a great gig.

I'm confident that, with his oceans of experience, if *The Man Of A Thousand Voices* had the flu, he could still wing it through a show he couldn't pull out of. He wouldn't have lost his patter, audience participation, bravado, repartee, and ability to react immediately to what's happening in the room, and incorporate and improvise it all into his act. He'd still score a home run.

Early in my career, I saw a girl singer, coughing and spluttering with a cold in the dressing room, go out and win over a sold-out, temperamental crowd using just these tools in lieu of a voice. She also flung out a hilarious put-down to a hectoring from a pisshead, that drew howls of laughter. This was particularly deft… the "drunken taunt" was imaginary and the others didn't hear it simply because it hadn't been said.

She didn't tackle a song until ten minutes into her set, by which time it didn't matter a jot that she just about croaked her way through *River Deep, Mountain High*. Thanks to her preparation and ample skills, she already had them in the palm of her hand.

It's called *"Stagecraft"*, and it can't be downloaded from an app, nor is there a crash course. It takes many hours' live work to get and hone, but once you have, it's a pivotal part of your armoury. It looks effortless and easy only because it's supposed to.

About a decade into my career, I received a flustered call from a lady that ran a Liberal Club:

"Hello.. is that Dave Dawson?", asked a nervous voice

"Yes", I said

"Oh dear, this is rather difficult" said the lady, uncomfortably.

"You see, I've been given your card by a lovely couple that use our club. They saw you perform and insist that I must book you. The trouble is... I know what with Equity and the Musician's Union there aren't supposed to be two entertainers working under the same name, but we had a Dave Dawson here years ago, and he was... oh, I just can't begin to tell you... His voice was very good but he was a shambles. Just awful. If our members confuse the two of you or if God forbid you're the same-"

"-Don't panic.. calm down....he got better", I interrupted

"God, I hope so", she replied, anxiously

"Look", I said. "I'll send you a poster, and underneath it write, '*New Improved Dave Dawson - Top Vocalist*'...

...Then underneath *Top Vocalist*, write...

"*This is not an instruction*'"

Chapter 25.
"Breaking up is easy to do"

After a standout night at a club, I phoned the Secretary for another booking. My only reservation about calling was he might want ten, which I didn't have to spare.

"Hi, it's Dave", I said. "Did you enjoy last night?!"

"Not half!", he replied. "The members are still going on about it, and we took more at the bar than we normally do in a week!"

"Excellent stuff", I said. "I'm just phoning to see when you wanted to book me in for next year"

"Oh no, you've misunderstood", said the Secretary. "We'll not be having you back Dave, I'm sorry"

"Eh?", I said

He explained that because I hadn't played there for a while, so many people turned up that they were queued round the side of the club, blocking the fire exit. The committee said it was a safety hazard and could shut them down, so they best not rebook me.

"Let me see if I've understood you correctly", I said, slowly.

"I'm so popular at your club that I can't play there again.."

"Yes", he said

I used to beat myself up over losing venues, but stopped when I resigned myself to the fact that it can happen for many reasons completely unconnected to the standard of my work.

❖❖❖❖

A pub dropped me after five years of great nights, saying I was "over the hill", which was a bit harsh, because everybody else that went there was, too... it was on an incline.

A regular mounted a dedicated campaign to oust me, even going to the intrepid lengths of sending the landlord letters under aliases, stating that if this woeful entertainer was rebooked, they'd never set foot in there again, and encourage his locals not to either. The publican, worried for his livelihood, caved in.

Was my act really that offensive? Don't be silly. The guy had asked my girlfriend out, *as I was performing*, and her angry rebuke had humiliated him so much that he couldn't stomach the possibility of ever facing her again... so he eradicated it.

❖❖❖❖

I lost a gig because of a *sixth* encore. A two hour afternoon job stretched on and I had another show to get to and was cutting it fine. They didn't care what I played, as long as it was fast.

With the crowd still going loopy, I had no choice but to switch down into first gear and sap the energy from the room with three slow ballads, or else not get off. I was everyone's best mate up to then, but lost the gig on the strength - or weakness - of that last ten minutes. I was cancelled for being "too dirgy"... it's always the last song they'll all be whistling on the way home.

❖❖❖❖

  Another time, under near identical circumstances, I had time for just one more encore, but half the crowd wanted a certain controversial *"black face"* 1920s singer, and the other half, Bad Manners. Technically I'd already finished, and couldn't appease both sides, so compromised by doing *Lip Up Fatty* in the style of Al Jolson. It went down a treat, being both very funny and just a muck about in my downtime to round off the set.

  It was just my bad luck that the guvnor, who'd been out all day and never seen me before, walked in right then, and thought this travesty to be my *actual act*. I lost all repeat dates.

This is like a keeper, who's made a hundred great saves, losing his place because the new manager has just turned up to see a fan punt the ball into an open goal as the team leave the pitch.

❖❖❖❖

  I did a club, trying to cater for a table of pensioners at one end and some youngsters at the other, by juggling between their preferred tastes. Rather than being congratulated for keeping everybody in, I was barred for *"not sticking to one thing"*.

❖❖❖❖

A gig went down the pan when I upset a squiffy old dear who requested her dear departed husband's favourite song, *Halfway To Paradise*. She burst into tears, so I went over to comfort her.

"I'm sorry.. you just remind me so much of him", she bawled.
"Sometimes when you play a song that was special to two people and one's died, it can be upsetting" I said, consoling her.
"Died?!", she said, blowing into her hanky and shaking her head vigorously. "Oh, I lost him alright, but he's not dead - he ran off with my best friend - I can't *find* 'im to kill 'im!!"

I've had men kiss me on the cheek with their arms around my neck saying *"Thanks"* for God knows what, after I've sung *I Left My Heart In San Francisco,* and others glare at me homicidally before thundering out of a cabaret gig during *Relight My Fire*. I haven't read the biography of every person in the audience, so I never know if a song will elevate or injure them.

Songs are multi-functional power tools, which is very unsettling for the handyman wielding them in public with a blindfold on.

❖❖❖❖

I played *Highway To Hell* at a devoutly religious Catholic care home specialising in looking after retired priests and nuns. I was unceremoniously ditched for "bringing evil music into their sanctuary". They had Max Bygraves on when I walked in though, and I can't think of anything more hellish than that.

Just to rub it in, they said Cliff Richard was more spiritual and befitting of their ambience, so I can only assume their Greatest Hits CD skipped at *Devil Woman*.

❖❖❖❖

I judged a fancy dress contest from the stage, awarding third prize to a Tina Turner in a leather skirt, and a spiky red wig, and telling her she could take it off now. Sadly for me, she'd actually just wandered in from another bar and it was her real hair, and she hadn't entered the competition. It was *Simply The Worst* mistake I've ever made, of this nature. I was never asked back.

❖❖❖❖

I was binned by a social club after a report that I couldn't sing. I asked who'd "filed" it, and if I could take notes from them. I hadn't had a lesson for years, so I was genuinely concerned that my technique was slipping. My voice sounded fine to me and nobody else had complained - but a fault may have been picked up by a fellow professional critiquing me on a night off.

"It's Jim", they said "... the window cleaner"
"Thanks, I'll leave it", I said

❖❖❖❖

I was playing an indoor graveyard to a dozen or so propped-up carcasses when half a ton of chav in a tracksuit shouted that she *"could sing better than that in the bath"*.

There'd been no let up from these plebs from the get-go. I cracked, turned off my gear, pulled up a chair and flumped into it with my head in my hands. A mocking voice asked,
 "Aww, what's he doing? Crying for his mummy?"
 "I'm so so sorry everyone", I said, through my palms, "but it's just the thought of…"
(I raised a finger and pointed it at the lardmass in the Adidas)
  "THAT, in the bath"

Losing that one was probably my fault.

Chapter 26.
"Elliott - 1, Mr. Clubland - Nil"

It was a charity event, in the upstairs function room of a lavish Country Club in the stock-broker belt. I agreed to perform two thirty minute spots, and during the interval my agent would bring on some local "talent". It was unpaid, and a favour.

After my first set, I heard someone slagging me off, deliberately within my earshot. He was a Yuppie-type in his forties, in chinos, a Saville Row shirt, and braces, talking to his identical Square Mile friends, all quaffing on flutes of champagne.

Now, a verbal lashing at a paid job is one thing, but I was doing this for nothing. I'd given up my free time, and fuel, to come out on a midweek evening. That's official partner diary space. If you want to fill it with anything else, there's visas involved, forms to fill in, formal interviews and all sorts. I don't want to get into it.

I'd been doing a good job, so was about to stroll over with ideas of chucking him off the balcony for a spot of bungee jumping off of his own suspenders, when my agent read my temper, grabbed me firmly by my wrist, and gestured *"No"*.
"Why not?", I said

"This is for a good cause David", she said. "...and he's a wanker. And if you start on him, he's loaded, so he'll probably hit you with that one thing that hurts more than a fist... litigation"

My blood bubbled as he prattled on, knowing I was listening:
"..So he has the spiel, he can 'work a crowd', and his voice is inoffensive enough, but he's getting on a bit isn't he? If he was that good, he'd have surely been on the telly by now?"
"No telly means no good" said one of his trader friends.
The first guy gestured towards his son, loitering nearby.
"Well, when our budding superstar gets up and struts his stuff I don't think we'll be seeing *Mister Clubland* for dust!!"

I was so rabid a passing off-duty vet tried to put me down.

My agent announced "our budding superstar", Elliott, and this very conceited little man of about fourteen strode onstage to overzealous applause from the FTSE 100 corner. With slicked back hair, and dressed in a matador jacket, satin shirt, bootlace tie, and snakeskin shoes, I was tempted to ask when the *Puerto Rican Pimp* look had suddenly become fashionable in Surbiton.

A karaoke *Lady in Red* started up, and he opened his mouth and spilled forth. He was flatter than an ice rink, and avoided more high notes than a barman warned about fake fifties. He was so appalling that I popped into town to clear my head...

...where I unfortunately witnessed a poor old lady being mugged.

A squad car arrived, and I was asked to go down to the station to provide a statement. I protested that I was compering at a local club and had to get back for my second spot... but unlike the caterwauling I'd just left, my words fell on deaf ears.

We were eventually allocated a room at Police HQ, and I gave a concise account of what I'd seen. I'd been gone an hour. There had been a few times when I'd wanted to flee a venue and run to a police station but, until now, never the other way around...

"Right, just a few more things", said the officer
"For fuck's sake", I whispered
"Are you oblivious as to the seriousness of this situation Mr. Dawson?!!", he snapped, losing his cool.

"Oh I'm fully aware of the magnitude, officer! I've fucked my agent off, probably been blacklisted by a big charity, and at this very second, some jumped up little tosser and his Hooray Henry nouveau riche parents and mates are all toasting themselves with spritzers and bragging about how little Elliott has been so stupendously first class that *Mister Clubland Singer* was too scared to come back!!!!", I shouted.

In my mind.

Chapter 27.
"I do what you do"

I was warned early in my career to beware of "floor singers" and not to indulge them. *"Compere Chris"* had me down as one, and was rightly scornful, until I allayed his fears. If a relative wants to get up at a family bash, then fine - I'm not a monster - as long as they don't mind using the "lurgy mic". It's a battered old Shure SM58 copy bought specifically for the purpose, that's had beer and crisp shrapnel spat in it by legions before them.

Also, if the dancefloor isn't packed and I won't lose momentum, I accommodate people that are nice, because what's the harm? *Sometimes,* I encounter a "freak of nature" great vocalist...

Lastly, if there's comedy potential that enhances the show, like a novelty song or funny vocal impressionist.. absolutely.

Other than that, they're a pain in the arse and can ruin your gig... and the bigger their attitude, the bigger the problem.

❖❖❖❖

I love seeing friends work, if I'm on the same patch. My mate was nearby once, so I popped in before my own gig. Bobby's a stand-up comedian too, with comebacks faster than 5G, so woe betide anyone trying to get the better of him.

He was mid-song when a floor singer swaggered onstage with a frantic *"kill the music"* sign. Such was his urgency that Bobby stopped his act, fearing a life-threatening emergency. The guy, shaking his head in astonishment said:

"It's five o'clock!"

Realising he was dealing with the one thing worse than a blazing building - a knobhead in the audience - Bobby said:

"If I want the time I've got a phone. Let me get back to work"

"*Everybody* knows I do a song at five o'clock before I go home for my dinner. It's song time. What are you playing at?"

"What am I, your warm up act? Hold on, I'll check the contract" said Bobby, reaching into his suit and unfolding the engagement terms, before melodramatically reading them aloud:

"Let's see. *The artist*... that's *me* by the way... not you.. just to be clear... *is engaged to perform three forty five minute spots between three and six pm*... No I can't see any-"

He slapped his forehead in pretend shock, ad libbing the rest: "God you're right I am so sorry, it's in the small print.. five pm... till three minutes past, artist required to vacate stage to allow for temporary substitution by complete pillock before his dinner!"

"Don't try my patience", the guy replied, as if it was *Bobby* taking the liberty. "The audience are expecting me"

Bobby looked around at a decidedly non-expectant audience.

"Really?", he said. "I can't see your gear. How long does it take for you to load in and set up. Will you be ready in ten seconds?"

"Don't try and be clever", snapped he interloper. "I'm using your equipment. You're just scared because I'm better than you"

"You versus me would be a chicken nugget in a cock fight, son. Now fuck off home, your Pot Noodle's getting cold"

❖❖❖❖

Floor singers and inadequate musicians often prowl our gigs and try to hijack them by harrassing us until we allow them up, in venues that won't book them because they're not up to scratch.

I yielded to one at a village pub. He was passable and obviously a local "face" so I permitted one song to bleed into five.

At the end he put out his hand and I moved to shake it but it was flattened upwards. He wanted paying!

"Can I help you?", I asked, quite irked

"I want my cut", he said, flippantly

"I was doing you a favour mate", I said

"I worked.. you owe me"

"OK", I said. "I'll come to one of your gigs and repay you with twenty minutes. Happy to even things out for you"

That was in 2004. I'm still waiting to redeem his refund.

❖❖❖❖

I acquiesced to another who arrived with his own minidiscs and faux-manager. She didn't ask but outright demanded that he be permitted to sing *"because it was his birthday"*, which I severely doubted. They sat right at the front, and she kept lifting her watch wrist up to me, glaring, until I finally allotted him a slot.

He showboated his way on to the stage, swiped my main mic off the stand and addressed the crowd as if it was *his own gig*:

"Before we go any further, how about a round of applause for this young man. He's going a grand job".

"Right, that's your lot", I said

❖❖❖❖

Another flopped on to my stage - it belongs to the venue but is mine when I'm contracted to appear on it - and grappled the mic from me, ranting that he had to sing *Summer Of '69*, because he knew it off by heart, honest. Then, two garbled lines in, he flounced into me, nearly toppling a speaker, and dribbled:

"Where'zzz the bloody wordzzzz?!"

"I'll just get a tin-opener!", I said. "They're in my head"

❖❖❖❖

The shoe's been on the other foot. Before I "turned pro", I was on a work jolly up aboard HMS Belfast, thrown by a client who pulled out the stops with real champagne and a weapons grade female-fronted jazz quartet. They were exceptional players, oozing dusty sophistication, and hiply attired.

The guitar player's creased, mahogany face placed him in his eighties, and he sat bolt upright and motionless, but for arms jerking up and down the neck and across the strings of his mirror bright, bottle-green Gretsch. As with all great jazz guitarists, his finger movements were imperceptible and looked static, giving the overall impression of a mannequin in crushed corduroy and suede with clockwork limbs. He was beyond cool.

They were playing to no one. Everybody was talking shop on deck or jammed in to the disco, leaving the band to resigned *"oh well"* shrugs at the end of each exquisitely presented number.

I spent the entire night being diligently unsociable, and the sole spectator to a masterclass. Towards the end, I called over, saying I was a semi-pro jazz vocalist and asking if I could sing a song?

The woman, in a blue taffeta ballgown, eyed me disparagingly, and said in a clipped tone that if I *was* what I claimed to be, then I should know a darned sight better than disrupt a fellow professional in the course of their work.

It was like a ticking off from a ragtime headmistress. I think I actually hung my head like a schoolboy and said,
"Yes, Miss"
....because she was dead right.

❖❖❖❖

A floor singer once sent his girlfriend over saying,
"Just to let you know, my boyfriend does what you do and he's coming up later to sing three songs"
"Just to let *him* know", I said. "don't send your girlfriend up to get the brush off. That's not fair. And if *you do what I do* ... it's Saturday night mate. Why aren't you working?"

I'll never let anyone wrench my mic away and tell me to move out the way so that they can "show me how it's done"...

... they never show us how it's done.

Chapter 28.
"Clockwork Soldiers"

In 2005, I sang in an East End pub on loan from 1973. You could barely see the flock wallpaper and wood panelling through air so laden with tobacco smoke it visibly draped from the plastic chandeliers down to the blood-red carpet. The clientele were all suavely dressed by the same era, in Kray Twin suits and *Carry On* film frocks, just for a night out in their local.

I banged out two spots of crooner and rock and roll standards; the musical score to their better days. I was accompanied by a highly proficient, comradely Scotsman hammering on the dusty house organ and belting out the odd throaty backing vocal, and a solid, if slightly grouchy-looking drummer behind a rudimentary kit balanced upon a rickety plateaux of covered beer crates.

The other members of this ragged one-night-only trio were getting on a bit, and I was growing accustomed to working with weathered old warriors, who'd ended up at the arse-end of "The Biz" after chiselling out minor but admirable legacies.

Some had served in one or two hit wonder 60s bands, while others had grafted in cabaret lounges, endured gruelling cruise ship schedules, performed in Big Bands, or worked as session players, cutting records with semi-famous names.

To "end up" in the pubs, is no cause for shame. In fact, I've met a few rock stars who envy the anonymity of a musician able to earn a good crust for a few hours' work and walk in and out of a venue unscathed, with no further demands made of them.

A gig is a gig to a jobbing muso. Unless you're "The Star", the only difference between playing the Royal Albert Hall or The Royal Oak is the size of the audience. The fee, backstage nibbles and changing facilities are often the same. I admired the resilience of any pedigree performer whose ego wasn't bruised by "slumming it" for their supper. As many point out to me,
"Well it's either this or a day job, and I don't like bosses!!"

After the first spot, we chatted. Sure enough, the percussionist had played for the BBC, on *Parkinson,* and nailed down the background beat to the conveyor belt on *The Generation Game.*

It was the chat with the organist I'll never forget, as I expected him to be cut from the same cloth. He assumed my musical taste to be Sinatra et al, given that I was adept at it, but I said I sang what paid the bills, and, anticipating the reference to be lost on him, said my favourite bands were "Prog" like King Crimson, and Cardiacs. Singing that would not get me rebooked at a pub borrowed from an episode of *Minder,* in Bethnal Green.

"Ah Yes, 'Prog Rock'", he replied with a laugh, tinged, I sensed, with a little sadness. "I pretty much invented that".

You meet a lot of "colourful characters" on the circuit, and get fed a lot of BS. The only connection a punter's *really* got to Sony is they own a PlayStation... but musos are also culpable.

I once overheard a wizened old bassist regale starry-eyed young rock fans with far-fetched revisions of his CV, including giving a big star his first break. The kids were amazed, asking if he was still in touch, but he said they'd not spoken for twenty five years. Trying to help, I interjected - the star was a personal friend. We could phone him *now* and do a low-budget *This Is Your Life*...
"*You've not heard from him since 1979... but here he is on the phone.. your old bass-playing friend*" etc etc.

I'd rumbled him. He eyed me with contempt, and tried to shoe me away with a scarcely perceptible *"fuck off"*, saying he'd mixed "our mutual friend" up with another star. It put my back up.
"What a stroke of luck, me being here", I said. "*He's* a personal friend too! Shall we give him a call as well?"

To this he told me to fuck off loudly, but by now his little tribe had smelt the cow poo and walked off...
(...don't tell anyone, but I *did* know the first star but was bluffing that I knew the other one. I knew he didn't, either.)

I appeared to have locked horns with yet another fantasist.

This one, however, wasn't turned down by Motorhead for being too wild, nor had The Kinks nicked the beermat he wrote "Waterloo Sunrise" on, and disguised it to avoid a legal battle.

No. This particular Elder Statesman was taking credit for an *entire musical genre* - a gargantuan force that dominated the 70s, via Pink Floyd, Genesis, and Jethro Tull. It still holds sway now, in the guise of heavyweights such as Radiohead, and Muse.

Hardcore Prog fans would have forgiven my cynicism in finding this declaration a tad hard to swallow. If I were sitting with one of the movement's primary trailblazers, it would surely be by his swimming pool, not some dingy pub with the bloke about to play *Tutti Frutti*... more importantly, *I'd know who he was.*

It's easy to call time on a charlatan spouting forth on your own *Mastermind* specialised subject. You just let them keep talking until they trip themselves up. But every detail in our intricate conversation, certainly chronologically, *all stacked up.*

Billy Ritchie said that his band, 1-2-3, had a residency at The Marquee in 1967, with Keith Emerson of The Nice and Emerson, Lake and Palmer, Rick Wakeman of Yes, and Robert Fripp of King Crimson all in the crowd, prior to forming their own year zero Prog bands. Jon Anderson, also from Yes, was the barman. He helped Billy in with his gear. 1-2-3 were his favourite band.

They were discovered by Brian Epstein, and toured with Jethro Tull. Billy flat-shared with the singer (tiring of him learning the flute), and Jeff Lynne from ELO. He formed a friendship with a kid that kipped on his floor, David Jones, who'd re-christened himself "Bowie". Billy introduced him to Jimi Hendrix.

Billy was also chucking "degree level" names into the mix, that only a "Prog aficionado" like myself would know… or, someone who was in the thick of the scene between 1966 and 1970.

During the second set I busked it a bit. My mind wasn't really on the job; I was more concerned with the questions.
"Who IS This Guy??? Why haven't I heard of him??"

I rushed home to Google him, and delved into forums, guerrilla websites, and blogs, all *100% vindicating Billy's version of events*. His innovations were the building blocks of prog - long, baroque pieces coloured with dramatic tempo changes, prodigious improvisation, complex time signatures and classical and jazz elements. The future prog rock luminaries at The Marquee weren't so much making notes as taking photocopies.

Just by chance, I was rebooked with Billy a week later. Our first encounter had ended warmly, so I didn't think it a liberty to say how suspicious I'd been of his previous claims, but I'd found them all to be true. If anything, he'd understated his case. I asked him how the hell he'd been erased from the history books.

"Aye", he said in that Lanarkshire brogue I'm now so familiar with because we've been mates for twenty years.
"Erased. I like that Dave. Erased"

Billy compares the circuit to a battlefield. Conscripts charge forward. Some rise through the ranks to be airlifted out onto manicured lawns, but it's also strewn with casualties of collapsed record labels, rotten timing, bad decisions, and horrendous management. And there are those like me that just forge on, dodging the bullets and escaping with just scratches.

Billy just had awful luck. 1-2-3 were renamed Clouds, and they altered their sound in a bid to become more commercial and break into the mainstream. Then Brian Epstein died, and his successor ploughed his efforts into a new trio called The Bee Gees instead. The prog rock templates were pilfered, and, Billy and 1-2-3, its pioneers, redacted from its heritage and ancestry.

Billy taught me that to go "back to the front" and fight on after nearly making it massive, took testicles of tellurium*...

..and that there were thousands of the wounded, just like him.

*"*Testicles of Tellurium*" isn't a prog album... but should be.

Chapter 29.
"The Clamp Its"

I was booked, in the early 2000s, as the support act for a well-known 80s singer in a nightclub, and was in fine voice in the soundcheck. That little warm-up pinned to my chest the shiniest medal of honour that can be bestowed to the second on the bill.

Come showtime, at the *exact instant* the announcer finished my intro and I was due on, the star's lackey nudged me in the ribs, saying my car was blocking access to a disabled space. If I didn't move it *now* it'd be clamped or towed away.

This is the oldest sabotage trick in the book, and, in terms of professional etiquette, way below the belt, because it's designed to disorientate the support act and "neutralise the threat". They still *have to* go onstage at that moment, and, if the ruse works, they'll be stressed out, fretting about all the nasties going on off-stage, and beyond their control, throughout their spot, throwing them off the job at hand. The ventriloquist at my first ever gig warned me of this manouvre but also told me to embrace it - it was sure-fire confirmation that you had the headliner rattled for fear of being outclassed. It meant you were a contender.

Recalling that advice was the catalyst, and knowing I'd got the main event's hackles up made me all the more raring to go... the opposite effect to that intended. Fully loaded with the safety catch off, I completely ignored his assistant and ran onstage, giving the audience both barrels. My car was fine, obviously.

My night was a one-off, but a friend had a near carbon copy situation, with a jaded 60s singer. Trevor was booked on a thirty date nationwide tour, as the warm-up. On the first night, narked at his maltreatment and attempts at derailing, he also "let 'em have it", blowing his gasket into a walloping performance.

The morning after pulverising his employer, he got a call from the tour manager, expecting copious praise, his own trailer, bigger print on the posters, and a pay rise... but no. He could look on the bright side though - no living out of suitcases for the next six weeks. He could sleep in his own bed - he was off the tour.

❖❖❖❖

(On the flipside, if a pub says it's OK to park on a double yellow because there are no traffic wardens around at that time of night, you'll *always* get a PCN on your windscreen wiping out half your fee. The buggers are like vampires. Some only *come out* at night)

Chapter 30.
"The Twilight Zone"

I was emailed by the secretary at a local tennis club, who'd seen my videos online and wanted to book me. She had an unusual and poetic sounding surname, so it stuck in my mind.

That evening, I played at a pub forty miles away and the relief manager, *who was only there for the day*, signed my receipt with that same surname. I mentioned the secretary that shared it, and it was her mum. Neither had discussed me with the other.

❖❖❖❖

A girl in Bournemouth asked for a song that I didn't know, so I learned it in my break and played it in the second half. I was a *hundred and fifty miles* north in Northampton the next night and played it again because I liked it. At the end, a guy told me it was his daughter's favourite. After a brief chat it transpired that he was definitely the father of the girl from Bournemouth.

This stuff happens *all the time*. I posted these accounts to some professional singers' forums, expecting with trepidation to be branded a nut or fibber. Instead, they prompted pages of similar examples, and a slew of commenters relieved that *"it's not just me"*. We all get these spooky coincidences *all the time*.

Chapter 31.
"Play Mr. Bojangles For Me"

It was in 2001, before social media. An elegant lady asked me for a card at a pub, because she wanted me to perform at her grandson's wedding. From close by, a female voice shouted:

"What do you want with him, you old slag?? Don't you get any ideas! Just fuck off before I do you!!"

Later, at 3am, the phone rang. My girlfriend had to be up at 6am for work. The voice on the other end was calm, but slurred.

"Why didn't you pay me any attention earlier? I thought we'd covered this off? And who was that old bag chatting you up?"

My girlfriend woke up. What's going on? The voice erupted.

"IS THAT OTHER SLUT THERE NOW?! DO YOU THINK I'M GOING TO TAKE THIS CRAP?? WHO DO YOU THI-"

I heard no more. I'd pulled the phone line from the socket.

My agent Dawn asked why I'd stopped answering my phones. I waited for calls to ring off, dialled 1471, and rang back. It was bad form if I had to be reached urgently, she said, and she was right. I explained all, waiting to be mocked. Instead she laughed,

"Oh diddums, come out from under the bed - you haven't *arrived* in this business darling until you've had a stalker!"

❖❖❖❖

The first encounter was nondescript. At least, to me. I'd been offstage literally seconds when she joined me at the bar. I nursed my half a Guinness, glad of a diversion before the dreaded equipment disassembly. She was timid and incredibly nervous.

Stumbling over her words, she said she loved my *Mr Bojangles* and had seen me live a few times. Was there any other talent in the family? Just cousin Rachel, I said, who was a brilliant and popular TV and theatre actress, and my uncle from The Who.

I confided that I only drank a pint and a half of Guinness on a gig night, and never before the first set, and that I adored Thai food, and Mickey Rourke - just like Rachel. I even told her that I found ironing therapeutic. Why I disclosed that, I have no idea.

It was just a little off-guard chatter with a coy fan... I thought.

She was at the next half dozen jobs I did in that area. I only saw her at three, but at all six I turned in the interval to find a fresh pint of Guinness by my amp. I started to get the jitters over it.

One day, she changed tact, announcing her presence by talking loudly upon entering the pub. She was always with different people but I never saw the same ones twice, so I wondered if she had a lot of mates, but perhaps I wasn't everyone's cup of tea. She cornered me in my break, blocking my exit, and in a way that I

took for brusque, but now see as contained wrath, asked:
 "Where should I join the line to talk to you, *Mr Unavailable*?"

 This was because, as belligerent as it sounds on my part, I was already going out of my way not to engage with her.

 Girls would pull at my sleeves between songs and say I'd better see to "my other half", who was in a right strop. I just shrugged as if to say *"What??"*, and carried on playing. You get a lot of strange comments while performing, that wash over you.

 At one gig, just as I went on, a barmaid said my cousin Rachel was on the phone, wanting to know about dropping a Mickey Rourke DVD off to me. She'd lost my landline and mobile. Was it OK to give them out and chat tomorrow? Of course, I said.

 I phoned Rachel the next day to tell her when I'd be in, and she asked what the hell I was talking about!

 The calls started that day. The first was casual but unsettling: "So when are you coming round to do my ironing? I know you find it relaxing. I could cook your favourite Thai while you do it"

 A guy doing this to a girl would be a creep. I was raging, but tried to stay restrained, telling her not to phone my home again. I was glad she liked my gigs, I said, but her deceit in getting my private numbers was not on. And, as I'd said, I was attached.

"I don't care. So what. I don't care"

"I've got to go"

"When are you coming over?"

"I'm not"

More calls came, day and night, at all hours. She got bolder in person, too, trapping me in my break at my next gig near her:

"Not so fast! You're not going anywhere.. Why are you ignoring me?! Why are you always trying to get me off the phone? And why don't you play me my *Mr. Bojangles* anymore?!!"

Her voice undulated between hissed and hysterical as she created a scene. One drinker mouthed *"lover's tiff"* to another, and I felt that nausea you get when you're mistaken as being "an item" with someone you fancy as much as a dose of swine flu.

"Do you think it's easy for me to get out?!", she ranted on. "I'm a single mother on a low income! I have to hire a babysitter, pay for the cab here and back, my drinks, *your* drinks!..."

Just for levity, I suggested she try telling U2 or Celine Dion to reimburse her train fare, babysitter and lunch bill if she saw them in concert, and see how that worked out. Then I edged past her out onto the street, and darted down a passageway. On my return, I sprinted to the relative safety of the stage, blanking her for the second half. She hung around until chucking out time, which I handled gallantly. I hid in the gents until she'd gone.

I was rewarded at 2am with a tirade that was tantamount to a death threat against me and *"that fucking bitch with you"*. Calls in this vein continued in a sporadic salvo, for weeks.

Stars can protect themselves against "crazies" with perimeter fencing, piranha-infested moats and huge bouncers. But if a loony takes a predatorial shine to a pub act, or someone has a grievance, there's no safe haven when the dates of your next appearances are displayed shouting *"Come And Get Me!!"*, from windows and "Upcoming Attractions" boards across the land...

She was affecting my business. My heart sank at the sight of upcoming gigs on her turf, in my calender. I'd turn away work she could hear about and get to, sometimes for lower paid jobs elsewhere. I primed the pubs that a nutcase had latched onto me, so apologies in advance for any disturbance she"ll cause. I seriously mulled over going out in her area under an alias - which rather defeats the object of having a following and a publican selling beer off the back of your name. She'd got to me. It was around then that I stopped picking up my phones.

Nobody could understand why I didn't tell her to fuck off or get an injunction, especially when I said I didn't want to hurt her feelings... even though she was shredding mine. My partner, quite reasonably, was pushing me to sort it out - before she did. I nearly phoned the police at one low point, but a singer with a similar "admirer" said nothing would happen until she'd "done something". How would I report it, then... via a ouija board?

Dawn had told me there was only one way to get rid of a stalker for good, but I was loathe to do it as it was horrible.

A few weeks later, she stomped through the door of my gig, flanked by two new friends. All I felt was the usual internal *"oh shit"*, and a foreboding queasiness. I was used to guessing her moods on arrival, and saw a steely, unshakable resolve.

She bought me my "usual", striking it on my table like a gavel. That was *yet another £3 spent on me,* she huffed... proving how unhinged she was now, as I never drank in my first session!

As I set up, she stooped over me, scolding. There was to be no more "namby-pambying about", she said. She'd done all the running in our "courtship" up to now, and wasn't leaving without this relationship well and truly underway. And, riled with my new "phone system", she was going to put me right about that, too. I was to make no plans for my interval. We were going to have a very serious chat. I just grunted, so wary of a "wrong" response, knowing she'd kick off and jeopardise the night.

For my break, I planned to wait for her to go to the loo, then hastily end the spot and do a runner to the car for a short drive.

My first set was fraught, because I knew if I didn't time things right there'd be an explosive confrontation. Luckily, when she went for a leak I was only four bars from the end of the number, so when I hit the last chord and jogged to the exit it didn't look too weird. I would have gotten away with it too, if it wasn't for her pesky mates. They were temps where she worked, who cornered me just yards from freedom, demanding "a word". "*Flaming Hell*", I thought... she's even got *them* trained, too.

As I said before, she brought different people each time, and I always wondered why. Tonight, the conundrum was solved. The first girl asked why I was "ignoring Veronica".

"Look, I don't know what she's told you", I said.
"You haven't said a word to her all night!", snapped the other one. "Would it cramp your style if the girlies knew you weren't available? I'd never put up with that if you were *my* fiance!"
"My....*what*??", I said in a shocked whisper.

The girls shot each other very uneasy glances. I tried to keep the shiver out of my voice but it was hard:
"She's not my fiance. She's just a fan who comes to my gigs... *ALL* my gigs, round here at any rate. Frankly, my girlfriend and I are close to breaking up over the nuisance calls to the house, and threats from that girl having a pee in the ladies now... I can't cope. I'm at the end of my rope. She's certifiable"

"Oh my God, we're so sorry", they replied, very softly

It wasn't their fault, and I hoped it wouldn't stop them coming to see me again, I said... adding that I now had to make myself scarce for the rest of my break. I *always* did when she turned up.

"Ok.. bye", they half-whispered.

Upon my return they'd gone. This was probably the only time her entourage had seen our "relationship" so clearly defined. Others may have sensed things hadn't sat right, deciding in their uneasiness not to attend any more gigs with her.

But *she* hadn't gone. She was sat alone, as still as a gargoyle, with a face like thunder, and unblinking eyes glued to the stage even before I was back on it. The guvnor eyed me as if to say, as good as he considered me, he didn't need this in his pub.

At the end, I was unplugging leads when I saw my nemesis charging at me like an elephant, for our "serious chat". I think I'd been bolstered by exposing her to her colleagues as I spoke, not taking my eyes off the cables I was wrapping up:
"You give me any trouble and I will tell this and every other gig I do just what you are. This all stops right now"
"Just what I am? Oh, you will now will you?!", she laughed, crossing her arms defiantly. This was particularly harrowing - I'd

have been less perturbed if she'd hadn't known "what she was".

I unwrapped my leads and plugged them back in. At long last, it was time to heed Dawn's horrid but vital advice.

"Ladies and gentleman... before I go..", I said into my mic.

The whole pub, knowing I'd finished, looked at me, puzzled. With the grandeur of a circus ringmaster I gestured towards her with both hands, and loudly exclaimed:

"Roll up, roll up, for your side-show! Here's my stalker standing right in front of me right now! Death threats! Telling virtual strangers we're getting married! Ringing me at home to scream abuse at me at three in the morning, making my *real* girlfriend nearly lose her job because she can't sleep! Damaging my career and swearing at people trying to book me for a wedding! ...THIS GIRL'S GOT IT ALL! ROLL UP, ROLL UP!"

As she left hurriedly, I yelled after her that she'd be hearing more of that little introduction! It was my new opening number!

...And that was the last I ever saw or heard of her. It was a cathartic moment, and I don't regret it a jot. I got my life back.

The elegant lady's wedding was lovely.

Chapter 32.
Night and Day

It was an Irish bar near Harrow, and a total slagheap. The first time I played there, I thought they were still in the middle of a refurb, as it resembled the decorating and dust sheet stage of *Changing Rooms*. Stale, uncollected glasses were glued to bare timber everywhere, the floor was like the moon landings, and it was derelict but for the swaying drinkers. The next time I rocked up it was even messier, so I realised that unless they were going for a *"demolition chic"* look, it was *always* a shithole.

It reminded me of another extended portaloo I binned off after being cancelled five times. Their last excuse was that they *were* having a refit, and when I drove past weeks later it was literally rubble - a pile of steaming bricks with men in hard hats buzzing around it. It was a definite improvement, and money well spent.

The day was monstrous from the off. I arrived just ten minutes before I was due on, after a hideous journey involving torrential rain, a flat tyre, dug up carriageways, and Ozzy Osbourne on my GPS nearly steering me into a duck-pond. Then I sprained my ankle sprinting my gear in, hoping to *just* make it if I worked like an octopus to get everything set up in three hundred seconds.

 The night before must have been pretty bad too. My leads were tangled into cable spaghetti - proving I've fled a gig, not left it - but I felt positive as the mass unknotted... only to discover the pool table hadn't been wheeled from the stage area, and a game of "killer eight-ball" with none potted was in full dawdle.

 The chaotic frame showed no signs of an imminent victor, as six Neanderthals in football shirts blindly ricocheted the cue ball around the cushions, and two more stuck fifty pee each down to play a "proper" game afterwards, goading me to object with "*watcha gonna do about it?*" glares, so that they could deck me.

 I finally got underway when they started on the Jagermeister shots and got so obliterated they forgot they were playing... but two songs in, a lumpen brute clambered onstage, snarling loudly that he'd rip my head off if I didn't let his ten year old nephew up to sing a rebel song about sending the British soldiers back home.

 By now, the impetus of the gruesome day had driven me over the brink. I fiercely retaliated, shouting that they came home in 2007, but he was probably too pickled to notice!

 He screamed that I was a *racist* and outstretched one fist towards me and pulled the other behind his ear, but didn't throw a punch... just standing there wavering like a statue of an archer after someone had nicked the bow and arrow, on a wonky plinth.

I'd grossly overstepped the mark. I was in serious danger, and millimetres from a pasting. The Jagermeister bunch smelt blood and circled, siding with the "Brit hater" residing in a country he abhorred. I looked pleadingly at the landlord to fish me from very choppy waters, only to hear him mumble to his missus that they should "wait until he hits him and take it from there".

After a brief stand-off, the tension miraculously dissolved, and, somehow, I made it through the three hours. The gravity of how close I'd come to serious injury only hit me when I got home. I fell through my front door in a heap and melted on the sofa, my body chugging in delayed shock like an old generator.

The next day, I was booked for an all-day festival in a massive beer garden, at a big Essex pub I played regularly. I turned up to find seven young bands on the bill, and must have still had the cloud of my near beating hanging over me, because people spotted that I seemed under the weather.

As day drew into evening I slowly realised there was no time for my two hour set... and all the bands were plugged in through a house P.A., leaving no space for my gear. I wasn't going to play.

This was obviously my swansong at the pub. My preferred fare there was rowdy "noughties" indie like Razorlight, The Killers, and Stereophonics, but my posters weren't up, and I was clearly now just yesterday's man - the sad middle-aged bloke playing covers of bands far more youthful than him, usurped by fresh blood far more fitted to the same material, and much better at it.

It was the final nail in the coffin of a shit weekend. I opted for a quiet exit, slowly skulking to the car to come home... only to be accosted by the management, asking where I was off to. I waffled something about obviously mixing up the dates in my diary as I wasn't advertised, but it was OK... my mistake.

"Don't be soft, Dave", he said. "We don't need posters for you. These bands are your *warm-up acts.* You're doing three quarters of an hour inside - full fee of course. You're a legend here, you're headlining... they'll all be out of the garden when you start"

Sure enough, the patio emptied and three hundred punters evacuated into the main pub, where I vented the previous day's hell into forty five blistering minutes. I tore the roof off the place and surfed on waves of love, slapping the dashboard all the way home in the car, shouting *"YES"*, and flicking mental V-Signs to the scum in North London that I'd never see again.

❖❖❖❖

The bride gathered up her dress at the end of my wedding gig, and ran up to me. The first dance had been Journey's *Don't Stop Believing,* which she spent with the groom not smooching but headbanging and playing air guitar. She put her bouquet down and gave me a tight hug, saying I'd made her day perfect.

Then her new husband strolled up and handed me a glass of bubbly, insisting I stay and celebrate with them at the evening reception, where I was treated like Royalty, then put up for free in a four poster bedroom with a tab for room service, followed by a full breakfast and use of the sauna in the morning.

Eight hours later, I was singing the same song at a Luton lager shanty, with plastic drug dealers jostling into me, using the stage as a short cut to the smoking shelter to sell bags of coke, and toe to toe with hooded yobs threatening, swear down, to vandalise my car and slash the tyres if I didn't turn this "heavy metal crap" off and put some drum 'n bass on right now, old man.

I see-sawed from darkness to light, hotel to hovel, sublime to subhuman, and 5 Star surroundings to £5 cannabis joints, often within the space of a night and day...

Chapter 33.
"It's a 'No' from me"

A few fleeting seconds on *The Michael Barrymore Show* aside, I've never appeared *"on the box"* as a performer, but it's been very close. I don't mean turning up on spec with thousands of others as just one more "moo" in a Cowell cattle market. These opportunities were all closed auditions, where you're summoned personally and allocated your own date and time.

❖❖❖❖

I landed a spot on a prime time TV Show, tributing a glam rock singer who was very famous at the time. I passed the audition, but my slot was given to someone else "doing" the same star, when the producers found out I was a professional. The show was for amateurs only. As a friend wryly put it, *"it seems a rocking horse can mimic a thoroughbred, but a real colt can't".*

❖❖❖❖

I earned a try out for the Jonathan Ross ITV talent show that discovered Charlotte Church, and was told I had it in the bag... only to louse it up on the day by selecting a different song to the one they'd wanted. Totally my fault.

❖❖❖❖

I landed a Channel 5 variety show and was given a date for live filming but the production company went into liquidation!

❖❖❖❖

I was called to two major TV talent shows but rejected both times for refusing to sign waivers permitting the producers to edit my appearances in any way they saw fit. *Four* professionals I knew had fallen victim to this, badly. They'd all given exemplary performances and gone down a storm with the audience, but the film had been cleverly recut to make it look like they'd bombed.

❖❖❖❖

In my late forties, I tested for a BBC light entertainment show, was on form, and knocked it out of the park in the audition. The panel green-lit me on the spot, and told me to expect a call to go through wardrobe, mugshots, and a timeline up to filming and transmission. I walked out on Cloud 9... *finally*.

I didn't hear another thing, and there was no way to chase it up. The showed aired, and a year later, out of the blue, I was called up to another closed audition, for the second series. There'd obviously been a huge cock-up and they were making amends.

I showed up and jumped a half a mile queue, telling one of the headset and clipboard children that mine was a requested audition. She checked her list. My name wasn't on it. They'd arsed it up *again*. I waited in line with the livestock, as cows to an abattoir, and shuffled six inches forward for three hours.

At 4pm I was summoned, striding purposefully into a suite taking up the whole tenth floor, with a vast plate glass wall offering panaronamic views of London's Capital. A young chap dressed in velvet trousers, and an "ironic" Iron Maiden T-shirt sat reading a paperback, next to a mousey looking teenaged girl. He glanced up, and asked me to confirm I was *"463"*.
"I'm Dave Dawson" I said. "You've called me back because I was supposed to be on telly last year but there was a mix-up"

He shrugged, strongly intimating I was lying, and curtly asked me to start when ready please. Unswayed, I did just that.

I was prepared and gave good song. Halfway through, *he went back to reading his paperback,* and at the end I heard him murmur to his minion that I was "fine" *but they already had someone my age on the show.* She nodded her servile assent.

Luckily the windows were all double-glazed, and there was no latch, or I could have been typing this from Parkhurst.

❖❖❖❖

I secured another closed audition for a more recent, massive, TV show, with just the small formality of some personal details to complete beforehand. I opened the letter and form, expecting to be quizzed on my background, training, and achievements, but instead all they wanted were banalities such as "*the zaniest thing I'd ever done*", "*a saucy secret I'd never told anyone before*", and "*what my friends <u>really</u> thought of me on a big night out*".

This all tragically coincided with me losing a close member of my family under circumstances the producers, and probably other hopefuls, would have leapt at exploiting. Compounded by the vapid questionnaire, I feared the whole thing would be turned into a "*he's doing it all in her memory*" circus.

I received an email the day after the audition, thanking me both for attending and for giving it my all, but informing me that unfortunately I'd been unsuccessful on this particular occasion as I "*wasn't quite what they were looking for*".

...The thing is... I'd already told them I wasn't interested.
...I hadn't turned up, and had given it my nothing.

Chapter 34.

"Pop Idle"

"Hello, Dave? You don't know me but I know you!", crackled the voice on my hands-free, as I hurtled up the M1.

It was the producer of a hugely popular touring musical. He'd been left in the lurch after a bust-up with a principal vocalist, who'd been trying to muscle into other cast members' songs to increase his own stage time... and downing around ten pints of strong lager in the "Green Room" after shows.

Oddly enough, I'd seen the show three times as I kept being put on the guest list (which *should* have set me to thinking!), and had singled this guy out as a lion would a weak gazelle. He was a prime specimen of how to decimate the last vestiges of a talent. He tore into heavyweight numbers with dulcet, bluesy wailing, and the timbre in his voice was soulful and warm in his mid-range... but when he grasped for the simplest notes just outside, he looked like he was straining to do a crap. I don't know about the back, but all that came out the front was a hiss, and when he needed power for a belting crescendo, a grainy rasp. He knew what he was doing... but had nothing to do it *with*.

I was envious. The production was superb, different every time, and looked fantastic fun. I knew it was right up my alley.

The third time I went, I was waylaid in the foyer before curtain up, by a punter from a local club I played at. He joked that I was only there to fire poison darts at the washed-up singer, from the stalls. Nonplussed, I asked what he meant. He was matey with the director, who told him this guy was on borrowed time, and when he next slipped up, a lad called Dave Dawson would fill the vacancy. I thought he was pulling my leg, but he was adamant... and slightly nervous that he might have spoken out of turn, as he thought it was common knowledge.

Now, all the pieces fell into place, and certainly explained the free tickets! The producer had heard glowing reports about my abilities, and how I could emulate three singers integral to the production. Crucially, he'd then come to see me perform *"on the quiet"* without introducing himself. *"I was in"*, he now told me. Please could I be at the theatre in Brighton at 10am the next day for costume fitting and run-throughs. We opened in a week.

I said I was very grateful, but it wasn't that cut and dried. I was a jobbing act on my way to a corporate job that very minute, with a full diary for the next year, and I had to have a serious think.
 "I don't think you understand son!!", he said on loudspeaker, as I pulled into a lay-by, with my head now spinning.

He said this was the phone-call I'd waited for since I started out. It wasn't an audition. He'd seen and heard all he needed to, and besides, he was in dead schtuck because of this muppet messing him about, and needed to fix this quick.

 "You'll look back on this…", he said. "You've toiled for it and here it is… this is your way out of the clubs, my boy. It's time"

 The guy was legit. I'd tried to "get in" with him before and knew he was a big hitter, not a bullshitter. He had a laudable habit of casting from the circuit, astutely considering this an honourable training ground demanding the same experience, stamina, and robust character as a relentless, ever-evolving theatre tour.

 Before being handed it on a silver platter, I'd have done all it took to secure this dream job; it was the natural progression. But I had it now, and was I ecstatic? All I could think of was the brutal schlepp, and years, it had taken me to scrape myself up to this position. Now I was being told to drop everything, cancel nearly two hundred gigs, and peeve off all my agents and venues, burning all my bridges if this show didn't work out.

 I wasn't worried about being out of my depth - the role was well within my skill set - but the "worst case" was too awful to contemplate. The wheels falling off. I'd return to no work, and have to get a "proper job" whilst trying to salvage the damage and make new contacts. With a few weeks' warning, I could have put my house in order, with a back-up plan. It would be uphill, but I wouldn't leave everyone in the brown stuff.

Alas, breaks in this industry come from left field and you start *tomorrow*. If I was giving a day-job the boot, I'd already be on the train to the seaside, but this was my business.

After a day's agonising deliberation, I turned him down. He was audibly gobsmacked, and I wasn't far behind him.

❖❖❖❖

Some years later, I was "discovered" in a pub by a major mover and shaker who was amazed I'd never been spotted before. My deserved break was long overdue and guaranteed, she said, and she vowed to get me it. I did some detective work on her, and my stomach churned with nerves. She was the real McCoy. I'll call her "Jackie McCoy", as I can't afford a lawyer.

"Jackie" phoned the next morning, saying she'd just launched another "unknown", so it was serendipitous that this "project" should float down from the Universe for her out of nowhere..

Jackie was devising a "gameplan", all the while still barraging me with acclaim and adulation. In the meantime, could I please post her a CD and some pics? I obediently did.

Forty eight hours later, there was "incredible news". A huge Svengali, Simon Fuller, had a forty five minute window open up in the Midlands on Monday week, so I had to be in Birmingham for an exclusive audition and interview... and make sure I was on tip-top form as this guy was one hard cookie. If I was as great as I was last weekend he'd be a pushover. I'd as good as made it.

The name rang a bell instantly as the man behind The Spice Girls and S-Club 7, who'd also managed Steven Tyler from Aerosmith, Amy Winehouse and... well, you name it, he was probably behind it. He also created *Pop Idol* and *American Idol*.

I frantically checked my diary and sighed *"Oh No"*. I had a very strenuous weekend leading up to my magical Cinderella moment - two hour shows on both the Friday and Saturday, three forty minute spots on Sunday lunchtime, and another two hours on the Sunday night. Come the day, I wouldn't be fresh as a daisy but still torpid and half-comatose with a shattered throat.

When I asked if we could possibly defer the meeting for a day or two, she recoiled as if I'd offered to sandpaper her Mercedes. *"Certainly not!"*, she half-screeched. One did not dictate to a magnate like this! This was my passport to the top and it could easily be revoked if I started effing about.

"Look, darling", she reasoned - it's one day's work if I offed the Sunday jobs. What's that next to the rest of my glittering career?

I phoned both venues and explained very subserviently, at less than a week's notice, that I had a possible big break and was desperately sorry but would they mind awfully if I rescheduled? My diary was so rammed though that it wouldn't be in the foreseeable future, but about three months hence.

They were decent people and said it was fine, and wished me luck, with one joking that I could repay them with a stretch limo and backstage passes to my first gig at the 02 Arena.

I swallowed the loss of earnings and a gallon of manuka honey on the day, rising at 6am to ensure optimum vocal ability. I was two hours and two thirds of the way up the M40, when my benefactor phoned. She was "so very sorry dearie", but Simon's had to fly to LA to pick up a gong, so he's had to postpone. He'll fit you in when he's back. Still very exciting though, wasn't it?

I was so angry I nearly turned green, swelled to three times my size and ripped through my shirt. I said that losing £350 in earnings and driving past Bicester Services in the pissing rain wasn't very exciting, thank you, and asked,

"When did he find out about this. Right this second??"

"Er...." she stuttered, and deflected the question, saying that, while she had me on the line, it wouldn't hurt to stick a few more irons in the fire, but my present promo pack wouldn't cut the mustard at this stratospheric level. I'll need to record a CD of more up to date songs, and get some new publicity shots as my current ones didn't do me justice... she'd book me a couple of days' studio time and a session with a top fashion photographer!

I'd also need a new wardrobe and a stylist to appeal to a wider market, and ideally a showreel video.

I asked who was paying for all this, and Jackie said *"initially"* I was, but it was an "investment in my future" and I had to make sacrifices... I'd get it all back when the momentum starts rolling.

"Bollocks to that", I said
"This is your big break, David. How much do you want this??", snapped my "new manager" down the phone line.
"Not that much", I sighed, wearily. I was too old to be told off.
"So you're happy to slog round the pubs and clubs for the rest of your life then, are you?!"
"Absolutely. It's a steady income and my diary's always full."
"You know what *your* trouble is don't you, my darling? You're too *lazy* to be a star!"
"You're quite right..", I said. "Just call me *Pop Idle*"

I've no doubt she rang off dismissing me as just another pub act who didn't "have it in them" to take the leap... although it's worth noting that as I'd never had any direct contact with Mr. Fuller, I couldn't guarantee this wasn't all bait to keep me on the hook, and she wasn't in fact full of crap.

Of course, if I'm approached now by anyone promising to put me in a glass coach and whisk me off to the Ball, I stop them in their tracks and tell them, no disrespect, but I've heard it all before... so I probably *have* missed a break or ten.

My career has been punctuated by many variations of what I've just recounted. I've given short shrift to Turkish hoteliers, "management tycoons", West End puppet masters, development deals, recording contracts and out and out bullshit artists, some with a screw loose. It's not a question of arrogance, or not having the cajones - it takes brass balls to be a solo act with any longevity. It's just that once I've seen how many hoops I have to jump through, I simply can't be arsed. And I'm too busy. And you can only have your plonker pulled so many times.

Not comprehending why an artist doesn't want to leave the circuit is as alien to me as asking a chartered surveyor why he's valuing semi-detacheds and not palaces, or extraterrestrials transmitting thoughtwaves to Leonardo DiCaprio, saying OK, he's got Earth sewn up, but why isn't he trying to make it *bigger* , starring in blockbusters for the rest of the Milky Way...

Chapter 35.

"Jump Leads"

The phone call was very friendly:

"Hi Dave! We saw you at that hotel last night. We'd love you to come and entertain the residents at our care home!"

"Good Lord", I thought. Was I really getting so ropey that people think I'm only fit for old folk who probably don't know what day it is? Or are they just trying their luck?'

I was offended to be asked, and politely declined. I knew I was on the bottom rung, but to accept a gig at a "venue" like this would be lowering the showbiz ladder down into the basement. I'd have to be on my last legs as an entertainer. Maybe in a few years' time if my prowess subsided, but certainly not yet.

It was meant to be though, because I was persuaded as a "one-off" favour, to play an unconnected home a few weeks later. I groaned as the date loomed, hoping there'd be no posters up advertising the "event". People I knew might spot them and think I'd hit the skids. Fingers crossed, it would cancel.

Even so, I did some homework constructing a suitable set. I looked at old time music hall, wartime and Flannagan and Allen stuff, but it all smacked a bit of cliché and *"that'll do"*... which led to a brainwave. Why waste my expansive catalogue of songs? There was scope for the antiques to sit alongside shinier pieces.

I reasoned that an eighty year old didn't stop listening to music when they were fifteen. I could easily slip in The Hollies, Bill Hailey and Bob Marley, and still evoke relatively youthful memories. Before I knew it, the day arrived and it was time to get the blasted thing over with and return to "proper gigs".

I'm not bigging myself up here. It was the songs that did it. But to see their effect on the residents, many of whom were lost within their execrable mental conditions and inanimate before I started the gig, was the first indicator that I wanted to excel in this field. Also, they were almost all day bookings, so didn't incur godawful late nights. It would be nice to have some weekend breakfasts again, that weren't in the afternoon!

The tunes seemed to nudge my audience on the shoulder like old friends that hadn't visited for a while, and their reactions were joyous. They roused. They became enlivened. Some were tapping their feet to the beat, others mouthing the lyrics or singing along raucously, and still others were wrestling themselves out of their armchairs to dance. The music wasn't obstructed by their dementia... it defied it. A time machine, teleporting passengers to happier times. Within two or three minutes the lounge was transformed into a place of celebration.

I can't delve into the psychology of that conversion; I just knew I was deeply affected by the sheer potency of recognisable melodies invigorating and connecting with elderly people, all with their own difficulties... and whereas at another gig I might just be background music, perhaps even a hindrance to disinterested drinkers at a distant table, here the dynamic was intimate, immediate and tremendously uplifting. Admittedly, I "only" earned 50% of what I could quote elsewhere, but as my spouse quite rightly never tires of reminding me:

"Your hourly rate next to a "real job" is beyond ridiculous"
It was also 0% aggro. A skip in a field of daisies, not landmines.

Where before I railed against "floor singers", in care homes they were actively encouraged, because they weren't show-offs, just people celebrating their younger selves. I bought more mics, and voices from the crowd were almost compulsory, making every performance an interactive group affair. Many people would shy away, saying they'd forgotten the lyrics, but as soon as their favourite songs played the words would come tumbling back.

Some people unaware of my resume ask if I play care homes

"because I'm not very good", and I suspect there *are* acts not competent enough for pubs or clubs who see these living rooms as an easy "halfway house" between their own, and the circuit.

"It doesn't matter what you play. It's not as if the old codgers are going anywhere" is a common hackneyed phrase.

The reality is a very demanding audience. You've got to give the best possible show every time. They aren't on a night out - I'm performing in their lounges, and they can be highly critical. If they don't like it, they've no qualms about asking to leave.

Being on a linear timeline to my audience is fascinating. We're all growing older and shuttling forward together, separated by a locked-in age difference. An elderly resident requesting *Stuck In The Middle* or *Ride A White Swan* would've been laughable when I started ten years ago. Now I perform them often. They're ingrained in the notch that our time has ratcheted its teeth onto.

In a decade from now, Depeche Mode and Human League will be to us what Manfred Mann and Herman's Hermits are to my current audience, and *Pretty Flamingo* and *Something Tells Me I'm Into Something Good* will be to the next generation what *You Are My Sunshine* and *Daisy, Daisy* are to mine. In 2050, some of us as *residents* will hear Pulp and Metallica performed by new entertainers who are yet to be born. *Master of Puppets* and *Disco 2000* will be our beloved relics, and *their* Stealer's Wheel and T-

Rex... and *White Cliffs of Dover* and *Hello Dolly* will be obselete - not even be a blip on the playlist.

As I approached middle age, with each revolution, my circuit was like an airport carousel burdened with ever heavier baggage. In that sense, discovering care home entertainment was my salvation. It rejuvenated my passion and reminded me of all the reasons why I wanted to get into this business in the first place. I often thought of *The Man of A Thousand Voices*, all those years ago, telling me to keep that spark in my eye as long as I could, and not let the circuit kick it out of me. Despite my efforts and determination to comply, it was by now closer to a dull ember.

One activities lady who booked me called my sessions "jump leads"... but they weren't just recharging *"the ressies"*, as we affectionately call them. My battery had nearly run flat, too.

Now I'd had a new one fitted and was raring to go again.

Chapter 36.

"I wish I knew a little bit more..."

The most perfect lament I've ever heard encapsulating the inner state of so many dementia and Alzheimer sufferers, came from an elderly man shuffling about on his walking frame in his slippers, in the communal lounge... he gracefully repeated the same mantra over and over again:

"I wish I knew a little bit more or a little bit less"

It was an erudite summation that could have been quoted from an existentialist work of art. A slight improvement in his faculties would have granted him acceptance, resignation, or control... or a slight lack, the mercy of having no awareness of his plight. As it was, he was stuck in limbo between the two. It touched me on a deep level, and helped me to understand the cruelty of this affliction, and how it might feel to suffer it.

❖❖❖❖

I can't illustrate better how little you can rely on past glories than the lady with dementia that took my hand after a recent show. She said I'd played every one of her favourite songs, and she'd never forget me for as long as she lived. I took some gear to the car with a warm, glowing feeling, then returned, whereupon she looked at me in my stagewear and asked cheerfully:

"Oh! Have we got music today?"

❖❖❖❖

I think it's because their job is often so bleak, that the humour of the staff is sharp, and stoic. An activities co-ordinator at one home, where the average resident age was ninety, once told me not to worry if there were fewer people clapping at the end of a gig than when I started. It wasn't anything I'd done wrong - it was just that sixty minutes is a long time in one of these places.

Another gave me the heads-up that a new client would soon be joining them in the lounge on my next visit, so please could I have some *Rudolph The Red-Nosed Reindeer* prepared for him.

"Hold on", I said. "I'm back in October"
"Don't worry, we made that mistake too", she said. "When he arrived in the Summer he was wearing a knitted snowman jumper. For Douglas, *every* day is Christmas"

Chapter 37.
"Deer Streets"

Of course, not all residents suffer from dementia. Many are completely "with it" and are in homes because they're unable to look after themselves, or, as one chap put it when I asked him:

"I'm just old, mate"

Interactions with residents, and some missteps on my part, have rewarded me with some highly amusing moments...

❖❖❖❖

"Thank God we've got a singer today. Last week we had a girl playing the harp. I know we're all close to the end but there's no need to rub it in. That's just taking the piss"

❖❖❖❖

"Ted's going to sing now... we've been rehearsing this in the car park all morning, haven't we, Ted?", I said as a gag

Ted sighed, then looked mournfully out of the window into the middle distance and, said over the mic,

"Take it from me mate. If I could make it to the fucking car park you wouldn't see me for fucking dust"

❖❖❖❖

I met a self-confessed "Acid Casualty" who'd been a roadie for a lot of 70s rock supergroups. During his illustrious career, he'd copiously partaken of many illicit pills, hallucinogens, "herbal remedies", and pharmaceuticals not on sale at Superdrug.

He was lucid, so his brain wasn't "fried", but might have been lightly poached. He'd drift off sometimes, mid-sentence... the years of non-prescription intake had clearly left their residue.

Excusing himself after a gig to watch some TV, he was told by a carer that his flat-screen was downloading some new channels at the moment, so may not be working just yet.

"Oh, don't worry about *that!*", he said, wheeling himself away. "Even when it's turned off, there's always something on *my* telly"

❖❖❖❖

I often play heavy metal songs in my soundcheck, just to amuse myself, and once picked out the intro to *Breaking The Law*.
"What shall we start with?", I said at showtime. A bit of Frank Ifield? Some Cockney songs? Or some Gracie Fields?"...

...A lady in her nineties, who I'd thought all this time to be sound asleep, with her eyes still closed, said:

"No, no, no…do the rest of that Judas Priest one… and then some Saxon if you've got any",

and then *did* drop off immediately, snoring, appropriately enough, like a Harley Davison on full throttle.

❖❖❖❖

"You should have heard the crap we had last week", laughed an acerbic old lady, referring to a duo that had just appeared there.

"If they'd have tried that on at my old British Legion, we'd have ripped them to pieces and raffled them off in the Meat Draw"

❖❖❖❖

I had my kit set up and one resident could only see the speakers and desk, as I was obscured around a corner, in an alcove, for a private birthday. After a few songs, family members took turns to recall stories over the mic about "our mum", with one meandering into a tedious anecdote that went on longer than a rambling audiobook. Suddenly, a disembodied voice cried out:

"TURN THE GRAMOPHONE OFF!! IT STARTED OFF NOT BAD BUT NOW THIS RECORD'S JUST TALKING SHIT!!"

❖❖❖❖

"That was really marvelous.. you really remind me of someone famous", said a jovial old chap, after my set.

I was very happy. I knew I was a pretty good Neil Diamond soundalike, and had experimented in the past with going out as a full tribute show. I'd bought the stage clothes - silver sequinned shirt and jacket - but the wig looked like two big dog ears, giving the overall impression of a basset hound in a space suit. If, as this resident intimated, I *naturally* looked like a well-known star without even dressing up, I could mine a rich seam. The pound signs reeled in my eyes. I needed to know more.

"That's great!", I said. "Who!"

"It will come to me in a minute", he said, musing hard

"OK, I just have to get my gear out", I said. "Have a think"

"I've got it!!!" he said on my return.

"Brilliant!", I exclaimed

"It's the butcher in Lyme Regis!!"

"I thought you said famous", I said, dolefully

"Oh everyone knew him there!", he said, sunnily.

"I suppose I could sing *Mince You've Been Gone"*, I said

"Best pork chops in Dorset!", he replied, with a thumbs up

❖❖❖❖

I cover a wide travelling radius and a lady who point blank

hated singers and took an extreme dislike to me personally used to raise hell every time I played at her home, and demand to be taken back to her room. I didn't take it to heart though.

She was moved by her family to another place twenty miles away that I also played. The first time I turned up when she was there, she closed her eyes and groaned, and said:
"Oh Jesus. There's two of him"

❖❖❖❖

After I sang a song, a resident's daughter mentioned it had been a TV theme tune in the 70s. It dawned on me that she was right, and for the rest of the show we were both straining our brains for which programme it originally came from.

We both gave up, and bade farewell in the car park. Sticking my guitar in the boot, it came back to me in a flash. I ran to her car and frantically tapped on the tinted window, motioning for her to wind it down, whereupon I shouted,
"THE DUKES OF HAZZARD!!" ...
... to be greeted by a terrified stranger in the driving seat, and, over my right shoulder, the sight of the "right car" driving away.

❖❖❖❖

At the end of a gig, somebody asked where I had to drive back to, and I answered that I lived in Salisbury.

"Where's that?", she asked

"WILTSHIRE!!" interjected one of the residents

"Yes, that's right", I said

"Where is it!!!", said the resident

"Well, between Berkshire, Hampshire and Dorset, really"

"Where is it???", repeated the resident, now quite curt

I repeated my answer.

"NO, WHERE'S MY BLOODY WHEELCHAIR!!!!"

❖❖❖❖

Before *We'll Meet Again*, I announced that we were finishing with a very important song as tomorrow was VE Day, and a resident said she wasn't very keen on it because her arms ached after having them up in the air too long.

"But Hetty", I said, "why did you have your arms in the air? We weren't surrendering. We won the war".

"Oh, sorry", she said. "I thought you meant *PE* day"

❖❖❖❖

During Covid I obviously couldn't do any physical shows, but got round the problem by doing "virtual gigs". I'd dress in my stage clobber, set up my gear in the living room and position my iPad centred on my head and shoulders, performing via Zoom or Skype. There'd be a window on the screen where I could see and hear the residents and on the whole it worked really well.

During one "gig", I kept overhearing the audience complaining that I wasn't moving around very much, so I started dancing about. They were still moaning that I was still a bit static, so I over-compensated by jigging around even more and waving my arms a lot. Although I was in the front room, I was expending more energy than I would during an "actual" gig.

Then, an old lady remarked that I looked a lot like Michael Caine, which was fair enough, as I wear similar glasses.

At the end of the show I was totally puffed out and went to turn my camera off, realising to my horror that I'd had it pointed to the reverse rather than in front. For half an hour, they'd been viewing my telly, which I'd paused on a clip from *Zulu*.

There's a post script to all of this. As the audiences could only ever see down to my navel, I must confess that at one gig I was late as I had problems connecting online, so although my top half was immaculately dressed in jacket, shirt, tie, and trilby hat... I only had my boxers and slippers on.

Not a lot of people know that.

❖❖❖❖

I played an elderly peoples' home in the West Country, billed as an "Old Time Sing-Along", and there wasn't a resident there below eighty. One lady at the front, who'd beamed through a show peppered with *Underneath The Arches, Side By Side* and the like, had a request. I expected to be asked for *On Mother Kelly's Doorstep* or *When You're Smiling*, but she threw me a massive curveball. In a warm Newcastle accent she said,

  "Does you have any Deer Streets?"

  I had no idea what Music Hall tune or artist she meant. Was it some obscure George Formby song? Or perhaps a double act she'd misremembered called "Ruminant Roads" or "Antelope Avenues"? I was absolutely flummoxed.

  "Sorry, but I don't know what *Deer Streets* is? Is it a highway for a stag??", I volunteered weakly. "Bambi Boulevards??", I continued, floundering. "I had bags of knowledge but they must have split on the way here.. Elk Parades??"

  I drew laughs from my clueless perseverance.

  "No, ya dafty...." she said, highly amused. "Dire Straits! Do you have any Mark Knopfler?"

  "Well, yes", I stammered, absolutely thrown. I picked my next words as carefully as a sweating character in a film deciding which wire they should cut to disarm the bomb:

"..but I'm impressed that a lady of your....distinction, and.. refined cultural tastes.. would know who Mark Knopfler was!"

"Well I should do", she said. "He's my son"

I tried, but not being in her offspring's league, my mangled *Sultans of Swing* sounded not like nimble fingers dancing on the fretboard, but the hooves of the aforementioned antlered beasts.

"I'll tell him about you", she said politely, when my toe-curling "interpretation" mercifully ended.

"Please don't", I replied, at least relieved that the carers' phones hadn't been held aloft, "*Making Movies*" of the atrocity.

Chapter 38.
John, Paul, Ringo and Bungle

  I was playing a very quaint lounge in an idyllic rustic manor house, in the countryside. It was one of those homes that's spacious while retaining the cosy feel of your own place. Ten residents were sat around me on comfy armchairs in a horseshoe, sipping tea from bone china cups as I performed by a dormant real fireplace. It was a black and white film in colour.

  A lady asked for some Beatles, after the resident opposite her requested the theme tune to the kids' TV programme *Rainbow* - a bizarre request which I thought would, pardon the pun, "go over the heads" of the other nine. She even insisted she knew all the words. Hopefully *A Hard Day's Night* would snap her out of her reveries of that morning's telly repeats.

  The trademark "*Clang!*" of that opening chord had the first lady instantly on her feet, shimmying away, supported by her Zimmer as she lip-synched every single bloody word.
  "Wow", I said at the end. "Did you like them at the time?"
  Her reply made me do a double take:
  "Well, I was on their payroll, so it was a ruddy good job I did. In

fact I think it was a contractual requirement!"

She'd worked for EMI's inner sanctum of half a dozen or so secretaries and receptionists straddling duel roles, seconded to answering thousands of letters begging for Beatles autographs. The "boys" popped in often, she said. When the fanmail rapidly became too much for the *Fab Four* to handle personally, this clandestine crew signed on their behalves, with full consent, of course, after practising their handwriting. Their forgeries - sorry, *"endorsed replicas"* - are a nightmare now for people selling them with authentification certificates on Ebay.

"If anyone's got a signed photograph of the "complete set", posted after 1964, it's got my squiggle on it", she laughed.

I asked who her favourite was and she tut-tutted, saying,
"Less of that. they were all lovely, they were all our boys"
OK, then, I persisted... her *least* favourite and upwards in ascending order? She looked at me with reproach, just as the "jazz headmistress" had when I'd asked to sing on HMS Belfast: "No. No I just won't", she said.
"That's why I asked for *Rainbow*!" said the other lady. "Ringo used to come and play with the house band for a laugh!"

She wore a BAFTA pendent. I hesitantly asked who she was.
"I created *Rainbow*", she replied. "And *Dramarama*. That was

Gary's first television appearance. I'm so very proud of him"

"Gary?"

"Oldman"

"I can't believe you've got a lady in there that forged The Beatles signatures with their permission, and another that invented Bungle and Zippy!" I said to the manager, after the show.

Without looking up from drafting the dinner menus, she said: "Did you see the lady doing the jigsaw in the dining room?.. She worked at Bletchley Park and helped crack the Enigma code"

I swear on Niles' Telecaster that this is the God's Honest Truth.

❖❖❖❖

I played a 90th birthday for a lovely man and had to shoehorn out of him what his old day job was. He finally told me he'd served his country in World War Two as a tail-gunner - survival rate, 30%, ever diminishing with every mission. He unfolded a brittle, gravy shaded photograph, held together with yellowed sellotape, of a debonair young prince in goggles and bomber jacket, leaning against his RAF Bomber with a pipe in his mouth.

I've detained myself for hours after gigs talking to scientists, film stars, fairground workers, circus performers, detectives, footballers, high court judges, TV actors, stuntmen, and Nazi-hunters, leaving courtyards and car parks in a surreal daze.

I'd walk into homes thinking that just because this was my four hundredth mile driven and fifth gig performed in four days, I must be some kind of Mediaeval travelling vagabond.

Then I'd meet jobbing musos who, before their fingers gnarled up, were working four to six hour sets, sometimes seven nights a week... one night in a brothel, the next on a moored Battleship, then Earl's Court, then someone's back garden, then an illegal drinking club, then a month on Egyptian cruises.

They'd done so for longer than I'd been alive, playing for the upper echelons of society – the aristocracy, oil magnates, multi-millionaire bankers and stock-traders, down to the lowest social strata of heroin addicts, murderers and estate agents. Alongside them, I'd only just stuck the gear in the car.

My encounters with all of these remarkable people made my boast of two Palladium shows and an uncle who'd been in The Who look a bit shit... but they shrunk my head... I've not had *"ears in different time zones"* for quite a while.

Epilogue.
"The Man Of A Thousand Venues"

A young lad messaged me on Facebook. He'd been watching me since he was a kid, because his parents were "fans", and had been taking him to my gigs for years, He was eager to pursue a career as a professional singer. He was determined to get it right.

His first show was in 2024. He'd been "killing it" at karaoke, and and wanted me to show him the ropes of the business. I offered to meet him at a gig and let him do a little fifteen minute spot.

He wasn't bad looking, and on this day was well-groomed, and immaculately turned-out. The lounge was packed, and despite the plaudits, he was very clearly petrified.

I'm in my fifties - which to him, a guy in his twenties, probably makes me seem seventy - and obviously a stalwart survivor of the *"Golden Club Era"* of the 90s. As far as he was concerned, his polished new train was being waved out of the platform to begin its trip, and mine was limping into the sidings at the end of the line, all rusted up, and destined for the breaker's yard... but I sensed that he wasn't without respect.

I was cramming eight gigs into the week, all at different venues. A voice, it was mine, boomed over room:

"And now ladies and gentleman, making his first appearance at Avon Green, please put your hands together for Dave Dawson*!!*"

I was on. He went out front and stood at the side. For an hour, he watched a sturdy old warhorse, conducting the audience like a composer, picking out spectators with a wave and a grin, and reeling them into his pocket. I must have jumped through fifty numbers covering just as many years.

I left the stage to appreciative applause and slipped into the dressing room, spotting him walk quietly in after me. I was friendly - I knew the score totally. I'd been in his shiny shoes, in a similar quandary, many years before.

"It's brilliant, a kid of your age being into real music" I said.

"Look me in the eye, mate" I said. He did.

"There it is. You've still got that spark there, mate. Now, you try and keep that as long as you can, mate. Don't let the circuit kick it out of ya, no matter what it chucks up. You've got to keep the good music going mate, or it'll die"

I'd stay and chat more, but I'm due onstage in an hour.

Printed in Great Britain
by Amazon